Victor Le Vine's Shorter Cameroon Writings, 1961-2007

Edited by
Milton Krieger

Langaa Research & Publishing CIG
Mankon, Bamenda

Publisher:
Langaa RPCIG
Langaa Research & Publishing Common Initiative Group
P.O. Box 902 Mankon
Bamenda
North West Region
Cameroon
Langaagrp@gmail.com
www.langaa-rpcig.net

Distributed in and outside N. America by African Books Collective
orders@africanbookscollective.com
www.africanbookcollective.com

ISBN: 9956-791-41-5

Acknowledgments

For permissions to reproduce original texts for this volume, the publisher and editor thank the following:

Washington University in St. Louis as copyright holder for materials from the Victor T. Le Vine Papers, University Archives, Department of Special Collections, Washington University Libraries, as follow:

"Eighteen Months after Independence: Is the Cameroun in Trouble?" (1961, Ch. 1 herein).

"Perspectives on Contemporary Politics in Cameroon" (1980, Ch 3 herein).

"Cameroon's April Revolt in Perspective" (1980, Ch. 4 herein).

"Crisis and Democratic Succession in Cameroon" (1992, Ch. 5 herein).

"Memorandum: Summary Background to the Bakassi Dispute (2007, Ch. 8 herein)

Copyright Clearance Center for "The Politics of Partition in Africa: The Cameroons and the Myth of Unification," Journal of International Affairs XVIII: 2 (1964), pp. 198-210 (Ch. 2 herein).

Jean-Germain Gros for "Ahmadou Ahidjo Revisited," Cameroon Politics and Society in Critical Perspectives (University Press of America, ISBN-10 0761825916), pp. 33-59 (Ch. 6 herein). Professor Gros edited this book, holds its copyright, and reserves rights for any full or partial future publication of Le Vine's contribution.

Lynne Rienner Publishers for Victor T. Le Vine, Politics in Francophone Africa (Lynne Rienner: Boulder, CO, 2004), pp. 310-313 (Ch. 7 herein).

Cover Photo: Richard Bjornson, Victor Le Vine, Dieter Keester, Marcien Towa and Hubert Mono Ndjana (Left to Right), at a reception hosted by Gilbert Andze Tsoungui, ca. 1980-1981. Photo Courtesy of Nathalie Le Vine.

Table of Contents

Table of Contents

Preface

This posthumous selection of Victor Le Vine's shorter writings on Cameroon, of which five appear in print for the first time in this volume, fully spans his half a century's scholarly career. A pioneer student as Cameroon's independence approached, few writers from beyond its borders arrived earlier, returned more often, spent more time there (roughly three years) and sustained their interest longer. None were more foundational in charting Cameroon's dramatic path to independence and beyond, and in linking the Cameroon experience to Africa's social science scholarship at large.

Victor's diverse background and a trilingual fluency that matched Cameroon's decades of colonization--born in Berlin in 1928 before his family moved to Paris in 1934 and then to the U.S.A. in 1940--account for his ready access to French and English-speaking parts of Cameroon and to German language materials. Only Harry Rudin among his predecessors and a few other scholars more recently shared such a capacity. Equally decisive was the mid- to late 1950s timing of Victor's University of California at Los Angeles apprenticeship in political science and African Studies. James Coleman's campus and national leadership in African Studies and Cold War-Sputnik era funding opportunities in a favorable foreign area studies niche (it was strategic, not just academic) gave Victor's years there a particular edge. Rene Lemarchand and Richard Sklar were among Victor's student colleagues who, like him, soon reached tropical Africa, excelled quickly (Victor was the first to complete the UCLA doctorate) and built notable careers. Victor's was at Washington University in St. Louis, 1961-2003. He remained active in African scholarship and advocacy until his death in 2010, at age eighty-one.

Le Vine first visited Cameroon for four months in 1959, a reconnaissance trip leading to his second and longest time there, for almost a year. It began eight months after the 1 January 1960 original Cameroon republic's independence day and ended three months before (re)unification day, 1 October 1961, when the French and British mandate and trust territories joined in a close approximation of what Germany had originally named Kamerun. Settling in Yaounde, he traveled widely within the original republic (at least as far north as Garoua) and throughout the still British-administered terrain. The graduate student research turned into a young scholar's seminal years, with his Ph.D. study published as *The Cameroons from Mandate to Independence* (1964) and recast as *The Cameroon Federal Republic* (1971), the premier academic appointment he never left, and enough "launch" experience and contacts to keep Victor in a high Africanist orbit for the rest of his life. As this book traces, he returned to Cameroon often enough (ranging from short lecture tours to a semester-long 1981-1982 Fulbright Fellowship) to sustain and expand his roster of print sources and informants, and thus to write what's sampled here. His mastery in Cameroon studies led to broader interests, travels, assignments and expertise, and ultimately to a signature publication in comparative African studies, *Politics in Francophone Africa* (2004).

Such was Victor's profile by the time of his death in 2010. His writings collected here expand Langaa's efforts to increase the readership of significant texts from and about

Africa, especially among Cameroonians. It is a labor of affection for the editor, one among many younger colleagues Victor helped introduce to Cameroon studies, in my case in 1990. I claim no special knowledge of Victor. We met just occasionally in the decade that followed, and for the last time in 1999. But we shared enough phone and digital correspondence over close to twenty years to fill some gaps through his academic and worldly advice on Cameroon politics and on the political asylum case work we both undertook, and for this relative cadet to serve as an interlocutor for Victor, a true elder.

The editorial purpose here is to introduce and reproduce eight of Le Vine's short writings in their separate chapters, bracketed by this preface and a conclusion. The volume will illuminate Cameroon's public life as he studied and reported it, from archives, rural pathways and urban pavements, and from his closer connections to its governing authorities between 1960 and 1990 than most scholars enjoyed. Previous writers on Cameroon were mostly from Europe, trained in a variety of academic disciplines or administrative posts, often as specialists in diverse parts of the colonized world. Le Vine's cumulative work conveys a sense of how, from 1960, a younger cohort of what became Cameroon specialists, from the United States and elsewhere, then increasingly from Cameroon itself, turned scholarship about this "African crossroads" country into a conspicuously important touchstone for African studies at large. What Le Vine wrote over almost fifty years continues to resonate in Cameroon's current circumstances, and will continue to do so whatever its twists and turns in the years ahead. The collection may be particularly useful for Cameroonians whose access to scholarship from abroad is limited. Those who want more than the sampling of his scholarship provided here can easily track his full publications roster by using standard print and online sources; this volume reproduces Le Vine texts in their original form, even if there are inconsistencies over time in matters like his use of italics, whether or not he placed an accent at the end of Yaounde, and the like.

To develop even Victor's cursory profile, as above and in what follows, incurred professional and personal debts to acknowledge before the text moves forward. First and foremost, my greatest debt is to his widow Nathalie, who helped this book develop as no one else could. They were students of Africa at UCLA and then newlyweds in Cameroon, 1960-1961, then were together in Ghana with their young children a decade later. Although Nathalie's dance career and family life curtailed her African experience thereafter, her recall of Victor's scholarly life was indispensable here, and the cover photograph from the family album was a special gift. Nathalie also cast a preliminary eye on roughly 100 boxes full of Victor's materials and then arranged my access to them through my second major benefactor, Washington University's archivist Sonya Rooney, who facilitated the scanning, transmission and inclusion in this volume of its five never previously published texts. I am also grateful to Victor's good friends and close colleagues for decades, Naomi Chazan and Rene Lemarchand, who read, clarified and enriched the editor's parts of this text.

It's problematic to work with a deceased major scholar's materials without benefit of that person's own selection, guidance and judgment. That's especially true for someone with Victor's experience, connections and panache, which are obvious to anyone who has read *Politics in Francophone Africa.* His casual stories and published writings not just on

Cameroon but on Africa at large include eye-witness accounts of the ceremonial mace hurled during a fierce dispute in Northern Nigeria's House of Assembly half a century ago and Muammar al-Qaddafi's hours-long speech a quarter century ago to a Ouagadougou audience including Thomas Sankara. The editor is knowledgeable about and privy to much less of Africa than his subject was, but believes that all the writings offered here were significant in their own place and time, and remain instructive and even provocative for Cameroon in the early 21st century, and (no doubt) beyond. Still, more than most writers' conventional professions of responsibility for errors certainly apply here, in hopes that (to quote the last line of Victor's introduction to *Politics in Francophone Africa*, p. 6, referring to its following 400+ pages) "they will be accepted as honest uncertainties, not evasions" (or worse).

Chapter 1

A Precarious Independence, 1961

Victor Le Vine completed his first Cameroon visit just before the original republic's formal birth, 1 January 1960, and returned in late 1960 for his longest period of research there. A benchmark passage he must have chosen carefully to place at lines 6-8 of his last book's last chapter (*Politics in Francophone Africa*, p. 337) records that New Years Day's perilous circumstances, as the Union des Populations Camerounaise (UPC) armed struggle pressed on against the successor government to France's: "Cameroon had become independent to the sound of rebel gunfire in the country's main cities and towns." A quick succession of events followed the edgy celebration: a 5 May 1960 referendum quite narrowly (60%-40%) adopting a constitution, general elections for the first national assembly, and the election that brought Ahidjo from a prime minister's to a president's office. This put constitutional formalities (if no more) in place. The November 1960 killing of Felix-Roland Moumie, the UPC's most formidable survivor, by French intelligence agents in Switzerland, stabilized but by no means resolved a delicate situation. Le Vine's second Cameroon sojourn, over nine months from late 1960 to mid-1961, included time in the still British-administered Southern Cameroons. On either side of the border, in three stages from February 1961, two much contested United Nations plebiscites determined which British terrain would become Nigerian and which Cameroonian, a July conference in Foumban followed by another in Yaounde and more private dealings negotiated the terms that would govern the soon to be joined

Cameroonians, and the federal republic was inaugurated 1 October 1961, just after Le Vine's departure.

From a typescript dated roughly two-thirds of the way through this longest of his Cameroon residencies, 8 April 1961, nearing the halfway point in time between the two plebiscites in (still) British Cameroons and the Foumban Conference, came Le Vine's first text offered here, unpublished until now. It summarized events unfolding, registered his immersion in them, and provides readers more than sixty years later a sense of the intense field experience he and other young pioneer scholars of African decolonization and independence were gaining. He recorded both the ebb of insurrectionary challenge and the countervailing jostle of political party and other domestic interest group formations, some encouraged, some suppressed, in the local and regional variations that complicated Ahidjo's assemblage of a working polity. His coverage beyond the domestic scene addressed potential disputes with Nigeria and the wider continental and overseas geopolitical ramifications of plans for regional and Pan-African unity and the Cold War's impact. Significantly for the future, in his profiles of John Ngu Foncha and Ahidjo, Le Vine traced the backdrop to what would simmer, then ultimately surface as the foreground conflict between the anglophone federal and the francophone (in Le Vine's later formulation) "imperial presidency" visions of the Cameroon state.

The 8 April text's first sentence judges that "Cameroun gives every indication of having passed the first, difficult post-independence stages with flying colors." But its last lines look forward to the Foumban Conference and beyond, predicting that "Mr. Foncha will be holding a good many aces…[he] will agree to the formation of a loose Cameroon federation. What he will do when the inevitable Federal elections come up is another question." Here and in writings that follow, Le Vine evaluated Cameroon's statecraft across the spectrum of possibilities. Readers half a century later, especially politically engaged Cameroonians, whether the knowledge is old or new to them, will recognize how the issues Le Vine articulated in his earliest scholarship continue to reverberate along a central fault line of the original governance structure.

Eighteen Months After Independence: Is The Cameroun In Trouble?

After sixteen months of independence the Cameroun gives every indication of having passed the first difficult post-independence stages with flying colors. The threat posed by the revolutionary, Conakry-based group headed by Dr. Felix Moumie appears to have vanished with the death of Dr. Moumie in Geneva. Except for a few marauding terrorist bands, the troubled Bamileke, Mungo, and Wouri areas are calm and agriculture in those sections has recovered considerably. Accords for technical and financial assistance have been signed with France, and sizeable development capital has been given and pledged by France, West Germany, the United Nations special African fund, the O.E.E.C., and other international agencies. The government party, headed by President Ahmadou Ahidjo, has consolidated its position by organizing sections in the southern and western parts of the country (being originally a northern-based party) and has absorbed two southern political parties, the Mouvement d'Action Nationale and Paysans Camerounais. The Cameroun has coordinated its activities in the international sphere with the so-called "African nations of French expression," also known as the "Brazzaville Twelve," and the group has laid plans for economic and political cooperation that cannot but benefit the Cameroun.

Despite the superficial brightness of the picture, there are signs that trouble may be brewing for the Ahidjo regime. The February, 1961 plebiscite in the British Cameroons appears to have created more problems than it solved, and it is these problems that have begun to plague President Ahidjo and his colleagues.

The February plebiscite, held under U.N. auspices, consisted, in fact, of two plebiscites, one in the northern and one in the southern sections of the Trust Territory. The alternatives put before the electorate were identical, that is, a choice between joining the Cameroun Republic or Nigeria. It will be recalled that the Southern Cameroons opted for the Cameroun Republic by a vote of 233,571 to 97,741, while the Northern Cameroons chose to join the Northern Region of Nigeria by a vote of 146,296 to 97,659.

The results in both sections of the Trust Territory came as a shock to the Cameroun Government. On the one hand, it had expected that the Northern Cameroons would choose the Republic, and on the other, it was astounded by the margin by which the pro-Cameroun vote won in the south. In both cases, the results were harbingers of difficulties ahead.

The Cameroun and the Northern Cameroons

The Cameroun Government's first reaction to the outcome of the Northern Cameroons plebiscite were that foul play had been committed, and that the results had been falsified. So wrought up did the Government become that it immediately lodged a complaint with the United Nations to the effect that the plebiscite did not represent the free choice of the Northern Camerounian voters. Both the Administering Authority (Great Britain) and the United Nations plebiscite supervisory team were charged with having permitted, even condoned, irregularities in the registration procedures , the conduct of the polling, and the counting of ballots. Moreover, Nigeria was accused of having sent 700 policemen into the area shortly before the plebiscite, ostensibly to intimidate the voters, forcing them, as it were, "to vote at the point of a bayonet." These and other charges were collected into a Government "white paper" and sent to the U.N.

Without going into the merits of the Cameroun's complaints, something outside the scope of our discussion, it is important to note their political effect. In the first place, it is possible that in its attempt to annul the Northern Cameroons vote, the Cameroun may find itself in an uncomfortable alliance with nations with which it has little in common or has even been on unfriendly terms in the past. Should the matter come to a vote before the U.N. General Assembly, as it might on a resolution to terminate the Trusteeship, the Cameroun will need the support of a third of the Assembly's members to block adoption. Thus far, only Brazil and the eleven other nations of the "Brazzaville Twelve" have agreed to support the Cameroun's position. But the Government has started to look elsewhere for votes. It sent Dr. Beybey Eyidi, a member of the opposition, to Ghana, Guinea, and Morocco to seek support, a remarkable development in the light of past events which have seen Ghana and Guinea and the Cameroun at swords' point on many different occasions. It will be recalled that Ghana and Guinea tried unsuccessfully to impose pre-independence elections on the Cameroun, and have consistently supported (in fact, continue to do so) the left-wing group formerly headed by Dr. Moumie, whose avowed purpose was, and still is, the fall of the Ahidjo regime. One can only guess what the Cameroun is willing to pay for these votes. Further, the issue may be one which the Soviet bloc might find useful as a means of furthering its own ambitions in Africa, as well as a new weapon with which to belabor the "colonialist" West.

There are yet other unpleasant vistas which the affair has opened up. The Cameroun may find that many of its friends, including the United States, will choose to support the U.N.

(i.e., the U.N. Commissioner's Report) rather than see that body suffer another loss to its already diminished prestige. A last, but not unimportant consideration is the Cameroun's future relations with its powerful neighbor, Nigeria. It is entirely possible that the affair may pollute the diplomatic air between the two countries for some time to come. Quiet efforts are now underway in diplomatic circles in Yaoundé to persuade the Cameroun Government to modify its adamant position and accept some sort of face-saving compromise before the affair comes to a vote in the U.N. If no such compromise can be worked out, the Cameroun stands to lose much more than just the Northern Cameroons.

Though the issue has been aired on the international level, the outcome of the case could profoundly affect the Government's position at home. The chances are good that the Cameroun will lose its case before the U.N.; if it does, it may discover that much of its popularity is gone and an alliance of former and present opposition forces confronting it. It is in this latter connection that the situation growing out of the Southern Cameroons plebiscite becomes crucial.

The Cameroun and the Southern Cameroons

The huge margin with which the Cameroun alternative won in the Southern Cameroons was undoubtedly mainly due to the skill with which Mr. John Foncha, the Southern Cameroon's Premier, managed the pre-plebiscite campaign. Mr. Foncha marshalled his forces and appeals so effectively that only seven of the twenty-six plebiscite districts tallied in favor of Nigeria. Everyone, including most of the politicians in Yaoundé, had thought the margin would be much smaller and were astonished by the results. It was an astonishment that was mixed with a good deal of apprehension at the vastly improved bargaining position the victory had given M. Foncha.

In essence, M. Foncha commands an electorate of about 350,000[1], a voting bloc large enough to be critical in any future elections to the legislature of the proposed United Kamerun Federation. It is small wonder, then, that M. Foncha has been privately and publicly wooed by both the Ahidjo Government and opposition groups in and out of the Cameroun National Assembly. Premier Foncha has had talks with Prince Douala Manga Bell, Dr. Beybey Eyidi, Daniel Kemajou, and other opposition leaders, and the fear is growing in Government circles that some sort of "western Coalition" (including the Bamileke, Mungo, Wouri, and Sanaga-Maritime departments, from which most of the opposition forces derive) may be in the making. If this is the case, the Government might stand to lose the support of a group of eighteen Bamileke deputies, whose alliance with the Government rests on the most tenuous of links. A "Western Coalition," with Foncha at its head, would have enough strength to topple the Ahidjo regime, even in the face of the Government's improved position elsewhere in the country. This is the vision which haunts the Government, and this is undoubtedly why the loss of the Northern Cameroons' 'electorate is so upsetting to Mr. Ahidjo and his colleagues. With the Northern Cameroons – if controlled by the Government party, as it most assuredly would be – an effective balance might have been struck to counter the voting potential of the Southern Cameroons. Without the northern area in Government hands, Mr. Foncha is in a good

[1] The size of the registration for the plebiscite. There are about 800,000 inhabitants in the Southern Cameroons.

position to demand, and get, virtually any arrangement he wishes, be it with the Government or the opposition forces.

One ought not underestimate the extent of Mr. Foncha's ambitions or the possible strength of a Foncha-led opposition. Not two weeks after the plebiscite, Mr. Foncha took pains to deny that he had any desire to become president of the future Cameroons (or Kamerun, or Cameroun) Federation. His denial sounded all too familiar to observers of the American political scene. He has, thus far, made it plain that he seeks a Cameroons Federation in which the Southern Cameroons would remain much the same as it is now, with the powers now held by the Administering Authority to be vested in the central government of the Federation. This is not an arrangement which is favored by President Ahidjo; as a matter of fact, when Foncha first suggested it in Yaoundé last year, he was turned down out of hand. But this, of course, was before the February plebiscite.

The long-awaited post-plebiscite conference has not yet met, nor has a date for it been agreed upon. A preliminary meeting involving British and Cameroun representat1ves foundered on the Cameroun's truculence over the Northern Cameroons issue. When the conference finally does meet however, Mr. Foncha will be holding a good many aces, and there is little doubt that he will play them with effect.

Observers here feel that, at least for now, Mr. Foncha will agree to the formation of a loose Cameroons federation. What he will do when the inevitable Federal elections come up is another question.

Chapter 2

Cameroon's "Invented Tradition," 1964

The accumulated 1959-1961 archive and field work became Le Vine's 1964 book on Cameroon at large, not just its governance, The *Cameroons from Mandate to Independence*, distinguished from other pioneer Cameroon 1960s publications, including David Gardinier's, Willard Johnson's and Engelbert Mveng's, by its comprehensive data and panoramic coverage. It was both anatomical and encyclopedic, and it made Le Vine the author of choice for chapters on Cameroon in close to a dozen anthologies on African politics appearing in English language publications covering the continent's independence era from this point forward to the mid-1980s. *The Cameroon Federal Republic* in 1971, shorter but still synoptic, was his well-timed capstone work on the first decade of the republic's history, before the next year's hastily organized referendum creating a "United Republic" changed not just the country's vocabulary but its entire trajectory.

The one short work reproduced here from this most intense period of his Cameroon scholarship, a somewhat atypical study, appeared as "The Politics of Partition: The Cameroons and the Myth of Unification" in *Journal of International Affairs* (18, 2) 1964. Here, Le Vine moved beyond empiricism to a survey of some major aspirational factors in early independent Africa: the efforts to reconfigure colonial groupings of its peoples, including not just those straddling arbitrary international borders but also those gathered under calculated management within colonies, and the broader schemes as independence emerged to establish regional cooperation and even Pan-African union.

Cameroon is part of the text's wider discussion, which compares half a dozen other partition experiences and their potential transformations through "reunification" projects with Cameroon's. Engaging the new scholarly literature of the time about "the invention of traditions" harking back to a "golden age" (he used the second term but not the first, which the editor considers appropriate and so interpolates, as a substitute for Le Vine's "legitimating myth" language), he examined the narratives developed to explain and justify such projects, and to convince the prospective communities being gathered of their efficacy. The Union of African States and The Mali Federation in West Africa and Rhodesia-Nyasaland's had already failed, leaving the Cameroon, Somali and Togo ventures still operative (Togo's was the closest to Cameroon's, given their parallel tri-colonial experiences). He found Cameroon's current "political symbology" exercise in Samson Adeoye George's 1956 nationalist rallying cry text and in what (from its German-era origin) the British scholar Edward Ardener shortly thereafter labeled the "Kamerun Idea." Le Vine dealt with both the clearly fictive and more historically grounded elements of this national unity vision. What, the text directly or indirectly asked, was the balance between coherent and incoherent, integrative and disintegrative features? Were the parts too varied to constitute a whole, or could this example among other such African assemblages be made to work?

This 1964 text was a precursor to Le Vine's 1964 and 1971 books, which offered substantial benchmark judgments about Cameroon's condition during the Federal Republic's decade. Those books' contextual summary, inserted here, will prepare readers for both this chapter's short selection and the next's, written sixteen years later. Le Vine's judgments in the two books, though hedged and cautious, were by and large positive about the economy's potential and the polity's performance as Ahidjo grew into the presidency. The 1971 book's summation of ten years' experience (pp. 179-185) was broadly optimistic: "Certainly in 1960, a restrained pessimism about Cameroon's future would have been the better part of predictive valor." Now, however: "On the economic front the situation looks quite hopeful…[and] it is the country's internal political picture that provides the best reasons for Cameroonians self-congratulation" against the grain of contrary evidence in the military coups and misrule recently surfacing in much of Africa. Although "the most difficult questions for the future lie in the social realm …[as] the country's ethnic groups are still relatively malintegrated" and in the still imponderable issue of the succession to Ahidjo, "here as elsewhere, the prospects are relatively good."

But, by contrast, the 1964 book's summary chapter on "Problems of Transition" (echoing Chapter 1 here) had previously warned that the republic's constitution, which Le Vine traced from its 1960 origins through its minor 1961 modifications creating the federation, was "a questionable Cameroun edition of the [French] Fifth Republic" and led him to "cast doubt [on it] as a unifying force" (pp. 226-227). Ahidjo's hastily organized referendum the year following the 1971 text turned Cameroon's Federal Republic into a United Republic. The delicate balance of forces stitched together across that fault line in the early 1960s, however well managed by Ahidjo twenty years forward, would eventually fray and Cameroon would experience its version of crises that long since had generated pessimism elsewhere in Africa.

Le Vine's own subsequent texts, and virtually all others of any substance, would reflect these tensions. The short 1964 article reproduced in this chapter offered no firm predictions about Cameroon's likelihood of success with this nation-building project, truly still in its infancy. But, as in most of the writings gathered here, current readers will recognize its application to and salience for the Cameroon that has emerged in the half century since, and can judge it accordingly.

The Politics of Partition in Africa: The Cameroons and the Myth of Unification [2]

I

There is a psychological immediacy, a poignancy in the evocation of a people arbitrarily sundered by alien intruders. It is an evocation that gives substance to demands for the ejection of the aliens and a restoration of past unities. It also helps to explain some of the appeal of Pan-Africanist doctrines whose cultural and historical aspects emphasize the evils of the colonial partition during the late nineteenth and early twentieth centuries. In any case, however unsatisfactory the colonial partition of the continent, it is the accepted basis of the present-day African state system. There are already some 31 African states (not including the Republic of South Africa), and that number is likely to increase to 35 or 36 before the end of 1965.

By professing to restore and re-emphasize the essential commonalities of negro Africa, politicians and intellectuals throughout the independent part of the continent have made the facts of the African partition common nationalist anti-themes.[3] Attempts to demonstrate that "negritude" (a

---

[2] The author is Assistant Professor of Political Science at Washington University in St. Louis. He has served as Research Associate at the African Studies Center at UCLA and as Consultant to the Department of Defense and the Peace Corps. He is the author of The Cameroun, From Mandate to Independence (1964) and a contributor to Political Groups and National Integration in Sub-Saharan Africa (1964).

[3] This is a theme which permeates a good deal of past and current nationalist writing in Africa. The most important body of literature in point is that dealing generally and specifically with Pan-Africanism. Three recent commentaries and collections on Pan Africanism can be consulted

doctrine elevated to a philosophy by Leopold Senghor) has no basis in empirical fact, that pre-colonial Africa knew no sense of unity beyond limited tribal or political bounds, that current nationalisms in Africa have come to be distinguished along the very territorial lines established during the partition are, of course, somewhat beside the point, though perhaps comforting to those who make them. The fact remains that many African leaders see no contradiction between nationalism and Pan-Africanism. It is often argued that the former is necessary to engage separate populations in the pressing tasks of political, social and economic development, and the latter, to foster the conditions for increasingly wider cooperation between African states. Indeed, for a few like Dr. Nkrumah, Pan-Africanism is symbolic of a stage when African states can be submerged in a continent-wide political union.[4]

Thus far, the most successful attempts at inter-state integration have been on functional and rhetorical rather than

---

for the most relevant ideas and documents: Phillipe Decraene, Le PanAfricanisme (Paris: Presses Universitaires de France, Collection "Que sais je?", 1959); Colin Legom, Pan-Africanism, a Short Political Guide (New York: Frederick A. Praeger, 1962); American Society of African Culture (ed.), Pan-Africanism Reconsidered (Berkeley: University of California Press, 1961).

[4] This is the conclusion he reaches in his Africa Must Unite (London: Heinemann, 1963) which was published to coincide with the opening of the Summit Conference of Independent African States held at Addis Ababa In May, 1963, Nkrumah's "brief" for a tighter political union of African states was implicitly rejected by the conference when it adopted the Charter of the Organization of African Unity, a much looser framework (or interstate cooperation than that envisioned in the book.

legal-constitutional levels.[5] Such organizations as the *Union Africaine et Malagache*, the *Organization Africaine et Malagache de Cooperation Economique* and the East African Common Services Organization have all proved to be valuable devices for developing a wide range of economic and political co-operation.[6] Such supranational frameworks as the Casablanca Treaty, the Pan-African Freedom Movement of East, Central, and Southern Africa (PAFMECSA), the frequent Heads of State conferences and the All-African Peoples Conferences have provided forums for the wider discussions of particular and common political problems. Not unimportantly, they have also given African leaders – in the process of defining common friends and denouncing common enemies –

---

[5] The distinction is similar to that made by Coleman and Apter to differentiate between what they call *suprastate political unification* (the creation of large-scale legal "sovereign" entities) and *interstate functional unification*, that is, the creation of interstate organizations designed to provide collaboration for common political, economic, social, and cultural tasks, but which do not involve the legal, constitutional merger of territorial units. David A. Apter and James S. Coleman, "Pan-Africanism or Nationalism in Africa." in AMSAC, Pan Africanism Reconsidered, op, cit., pp. 82-83 and passim.

[6] Since the burden of this article deals with the activities of independent African states, no mention has been made of either of the two great French African administrative federations, French West Africa, (AOF, Afrique Occidentale Française) and French Equatorial Africa (AEF, Afrique Equatorial Française). They provided the experience of inter-territorial cooperation that made possible such organizations as the Mali Federation the Council of the Entente the still amorphous Union of Equatorial African States and the Afro-Malagasy Union of Economic Cooperation (until March, 1964, the Afro-Malagasy Union and its component organizations).

opportunities for mutual reinforcement, reassurance and catharsis.[7]

Attempts at territorial union on constitutional-legal-political levels have been less successful. The Union of African States(Ghana-Guinea-Mali), born amid great fanfare in 1960, never progressed much beyond the rhetoric that accompanied its formation, and was quietly dissolved soon after the Heads of State meeting at Addis Ababa in May, 1963. The Mali Federation, formed in 1959, and originally designed to include all French-speaking African states, soon lost two of its four founding members (Dahomey and Upper Volta), and collapsed when the remaining members(Senegal and the Republic of Soudan, now the Republic of Mali)fell into acrimonious disagreement in 1960. The Federation of Rhodesia and Nyasaland, upon which the British Government and the white settlers in East Africa had placed their hopes for the evolution of a bi-racial "partnership," foundered on the rocks of hostile African leaders who saw the "partnership"-to use an oft-repeated but nonetheless trenchant phrase-as the "partnership between horse and rider," with themselves in the subordinate role. British Togoland, in a UN-supervised plebiscite in 1956, voted to integrate with Ghana, rather than with French Togoland, with which it had once shared common identity as the German Togoland Protectorate [8]

---

[7] The psychological functions of the international conference have only been peripherally explored to date. See, for example. Chadwick Alger, "Non-resolution consequences of the United Nations and their effect on international conflict," The Journal of Conflict Resolution, Vol. V, No. 2 (June, 1961), pp. 128-145.

[8] James S. Coleman, "Togoland," International Conciliation, No. 509) (Sept., 1956).

Thus far, only three major ventures in territorial integration have been crowned with any measure of success: the unification of British Togoland with Ghana, the merger of the British and former Italian Somalilands to form the unitary Republic of Somali and the "reunification" of the British Southern Cameroons with the Cameroun Republic, forming the present Cameroon Federal Republic. The Ghana-British Togoland merger capped almost forty years of de facto administrative union, Ewe tribal objections notwithstanding. Crucial to the union of the Somalilands was the almost complete ethnic commonality of the two territories. The Cameroon case is somewhat more complex. A closer look at the partition and "reunification" of the two Cameroons may; in fact, suggest some hypotheses to explain the failure of past attempts at territorial integration in Africa, as well as to clarify the political symbology of partition and unification.

II

On July 14, 1884, Gustav Nachtigal, lately German Imperial Consul in Tunis, hoisted the German flag over what is now Douala, creating the protectorate of Kamerun. Thirty years later, the First World War saw the military conquest of Kamerun by British, French and Belgian forces, and the de facto division of the protectorate into two parts, one adjoining Nigeria (comprising roughly one-fifth of the area of the old Kamerun) and ruled by Britain, and the other (four-fifths), ruled by France. The division was ratified by the Versailles treaties, and the two territories subsequently (1922) became mandates of the League of Nations under the respective administrations of Britain and France. Following the League's formal dissolution in 1946, the two mandates were converted into United Nations Trusteeships that lasted until the French Cameroun became independent on January 1, 1960, and the southern section of the British Cameroons united with the Cameroun Republic on October 1, 1961 to form the Cameroon Federal Republic. The merger was the principal outcome of plebiscites conducted by the United Nations in the two parts of the British Cameroons. On February 11, 1961, the voters in the Southern Cameroons overwhelmingly opted to join the Cameroun Republic; a sizeable majority in the Northern Cameroons voted for union with Nigeria (effected in July of that same year).[9] The merger of the Southern British Cameroons and the Cameroun Republic was regarded by nationalists on both sides of the old frontier as the culmination of a long struggle to realize what had come to be a goal espoused by almost all Cameroonian intellectuals, the "reunification" of Kamerun.

More than three years have passed since "reunification" was achieved, and the prospects for the continued existence of the federation are still reasonably good, though the facts would seem to argue the other way.[10] For example, the

---

[9] The United Nations plebiscites in the Cameroons are discussed by this writer in "Calm Before the Storm in Cameroun," Africa Report, Vol. VI, NO.5 (May, 1961), pp. 3-4; and by Reuben Fredin, "Flies in the Trusteeship Ointment," American Universities Field Staff Reports (Feb., 1961). The relevant official document is Report of the United Nations Plebiscite Commissioner for the Cameroons under United Kingdom Administration. Plebiscites in the southern and northern parts of the Territory. on 11 and 12 February 1961 (U.N. Doc. A/4717) New York, 1961.

[10] For an optimistic view of the Cameroon's prospects, see the articles by Claude E. Welsh, Jr. in West Africa, Nos. 2420-2423 (Oct.19-Nov. 9. 1963), pp. 1175, 1213, 1241, 1271, which review the first two years of the federation's existence.

Cameroun lacks the elements of ethnic community that binds the Somalis; the federation encompasses an almost unbelievable linguistic and cultural diversity: there are probably over 200 identifiable ethnic groups. Moreover, forty years of separate European control have given rise to deeply rooted economic, educational, legal and administrative institutions and habits. Given a situation of diversity in which fissiparous tendencies could well prevail over integrative forces, the cement that binds the two Cameroons must be sought in other contexts. One of the most important is the area of Cameroonian nationalist ideology, in particular the mythology of "reunification" -what Edwin Ardener has labelled "the Kamerun Idea."[11]

III

> I know that because of the two different institutions that have grown side by side in our country sceptics [sic] will doubt the possibility of a Kamerun merged as a united country. I can see traitors wondering what they will get if the two sections are joined together. I can see feebleminded people trembling at the thought of having to face this gigantic problem of welding the two cultures. British and French, into a third that must emerge from the unification of the two sections. In answer to these doubts I can say only one thing. that every event that has surrounded the existence of our people as a community has contributed in all ways to maintaining the identity of the people of Kamerun. When the Germans carved it out and gave it the political expression which we now know to be Kamerun, the wars came-two world wars-the

[11] Edwin Ardener, "The Kamerun Idea," *West Africa*, No. 2139 (June 7, 1958), p. 533; idem, No. 2142 (June 24, 1958), p. 559.

> country was tom in two. In later years the British section was tom in two again, and yet in the first act of partition which was sanctioned by the League of Nations, the country in both sections was called Kamerun, even the agreement by which they were administered as mandated territories. In later years, when the mandate was changed into the Trusteeship system, the two sections are still called Cameroons/Cameroun in each case. When the British section was further cut in two, even that section which chose to remain in Northern Nigeria continues to be called Cameroons, and the Southern Section is still called Cameroons. No matter what we do. no matter how we have tried, no matter how our enemies have tried, they have not succeeded in eliminating that one word which is the symbol of the unity of the country of Kamerun. It is the foundation of our existence and it is upon that I hope and pray that we shall build our nation.[12]

The selection is from a pamphlet, written in 1956 by Samson Adeoye George, one of the leaders of a small band of Southern Cameroon intellectuals who in the late 1940's first raised the issue discussed by the pamphlet, *Kamerun (Unification)*. The quotation is of particular interest because it pulls together most of the important elements of the Kamerun myth, elements which, in turn, enabled "reunification" to be used as a popular political symbol by almost all Cameroon nationalists in both the English- and French-speaking territories.

On closer examination, the "Kamerun" myth can be seen as an elaboration on and a re-interpretation of the historical facts of the German protectorate. There are two distinct

---

[12] S. A. George, *Kamerun (Unification)* (London: 1956), pp. 26-27.

facets to the myth. The first is that by the act of "carving it out," the Germans gave "political expression" to the Kamerun. In the context of George's discussion, the phraseology takes on important implications: "Kamerun" community pre-existed the German coming, but it had no definable political shape until the Germans gave it "expression." This connection, incidentally, helps to explain the widespread use of the German spelling (Kamerun) in nationalist literature and in the names of nationalist groups and parties. The Kamerun National Democratic Party and the One Kamerun parties in the West Cameroon (former British Cameroons), for example, deliberately adopted the German spelling to symbolize their support for the unification goal.

The second myth is that "the country was tom in two" following the two world wars. Not only George, but almost all Cameroon nationalists have contended that by the time the First World War broke out, the Kamerun was a "country" or a "nation," and that its subsequent partition by the Allies represented the cruel division of a self-conscious political community. The most important nationalist group in the French Cameroun, the Union des Populations du Cameroun (UPC), even adopted as doctrine a further elaboration of this thesis. The UPC contended that at the outbreak of war in 1914, the German treaty of annexation, having been signed to cover only a 30 year period from 1884, lapsed, and that thereupon the Kamerun became "juridical independent."[13] The UPC argument, of course, had the effect of permitting nationalists to contend that the Anglo-French partition was not only morally reprehensible but illegal as well.

---

[13] See. for example, the report of "a Group of Progressive Kamerunian Students," circulated to the delegates of the Sixth World Youth Festival, Moscow, 1957.

That the "Kamerun idea" is in fact myth is clear from the facts themselves. "In 1984," maintains Adalbert Ozona, "the 'Cameroun' did not exist ... either as a political or territorial entity ..."[14] The trading villages around the estuary of what is now known as the Wouri River, inhabited by the Douala -- then perhaps numbering at most some 20,000 – plus several trading stations on the coast southward and to the north were all that the European world knew of the area. "Kamerun" itself is the German transliteration of the Portuguese "Camaroes." "Rio dos Camaroes"-River of Shrimps-was the name given to the Wouri by Portuguese sailors, the first Europeans to record their penetration of the river. The Portuguese entered the Gulf of Guinea in 1471 and, struck by the innumerable whitish crustaceans found in one of the coastal rivers, named the whole estuary in remembrance of the event. It is interesting to note that the Portuguese were better sailors than marine biologists. What they saw were a variety of crayfish, not shrimp, that only appear in the Wouri at odd intervals. In any event, the several permutations of Cameroes (Camerún in Spanish, Cameroons in English, Cameroun in French) came subsequently to be applied to the cluster of trading towns upriver (Cameroon-Town, now Douala), to the adjacent coast and to the nearby sporadic volcano that dominates both river and coast. Even this spread of the name did not occur until comparatively late. Up to the beginning of the nineteenth century only the estuary and the river were thus identified; the mountain and the populations near the river were still known by such names as the Ambozes, Dwala or Calbongos.

---

[14] A. Owona, "Comment les Allemands ont mis la main sur le Cameroun," *Revue Camerounaise*, Année, NO.10, (July-Aug., 1959), p. v.

It is also clear that the German treaty of protection signed by "Kings" Bell and Akwa and various other Douala chiefs and notables was intended to bind only the Douala. If the treaty had been meant to apply otherwise, there would have been no need for Nachtigal to seek comparable agreements with several chiefs along the southward coast and raise the German flag over the trading stations at Malimba, Klein-Batanga, Kribi, Rio Benito and Bapuko. Moreover, nothing in the treaty permits of the interpretation that "the territory called Kamerun" extended anywhere beyond the limits of the Douala villages. It certainly did not extend, at least in 1884, to the British Missionary Settlement at Victoria, which had been claimed for Britain by Consul E. H. Hewett a few days before the Germans took over Douala. And most certainly it did not cover the inland and coastal lands occupied by such groups as the Bakweri, Bassa, Bulu and Beti, all on uneasy terms with the Douala and suspicious of the Germans, It must also be added that the Treaty of 1884 signed in Cameroon-Town--only' one, albeit one of the most important, of a host of such agreements concluded by the Germans with African chiefs during this period--contains nothing to substantiate the claim that it was limited to operate for no more than 30 years. Not even the vague wording of Article 5 could be read to provide for such a limitation: "During the early period of the administration here, our local customs and usages shall be respected."[15]

It is clear beyond doubt that there was no "Kamerun" before the Germans came. Even the Douala, who later came to claim the whole of the protectorate as theirs "since time immemorial," could trace their presence in the area back no further than the seventeenth century when they "either

---

[15] Ibid; pp. xxii-xxx. passim.

conquered or assimilated the indigenous Malimba and Bassa peoples.[16] Moreover, the Douala had not acquired the centralized political systems that might have given them a sense of identification beyond their villages and clan groupings: the titles of "King" enjoyed by their chiefs were more honorary than real Their control of the limited area around the estuary of the Rio dos Camaroes was due primarily to their useful middleman position in the slave trade and because European traders had provided them with firearms to keep their hostile enemies at bay.

In 1884 the rest of what is now the Cameroon was inhabited by a multiplicity of tribal groups having little in common with one another, but sharing a general suspicion of and hostility to strangers. Only in the Cameroon north, beyond the tropical rainforest, was there any sense of political cohesion, but it was the cohesion imposed by the Fulani conquests of the early nineteenth century which converted such towns as Ngaoundere, Garoua, Maroua and Yagoua, into outposts of the Emirate of Yola, itself a feudatory of Sokoto and Kano. It may be added that the Germans could not claim full control of the protectorate until 1911; as late as 1889 they had not proceeded beyond Yaounde.

When the Germans were finally driven from the field in 1916, the resulting partition of the protectorate between France and Britain meant little more for most of the inhabitants than the substitution of one European ruler for another, and that only in the degree to which the Germans, French or British had managed to penetrate local cultures or work through indigenous chiefs. Only in the Kamerun south was there any sense of the existence of "Kamerun," and this

---

16 "Petition by Willian Ganty of August 21, 1931" to the League of Nations Permanent Mandates Commission.

was something that could only be found among those Douala, Bassa, Bulu, Bakwiri or Beti who had received mission education or who spoke German to any extent. There is, in short, little to suggest that "a Kamerun nation" was "tom" or "dismembered" by its second wave of colonial rulers. What occurred was a political transaction in which the indigenous population was not consulted. With the exception of a small number that had come to identify with the Germans or who had developed a stake in German rule, most Cameroonians were only minimally or not at all involved in the partition and change of administration. A single group, the Douala, hailed the end of the German protectorate, and they rejoiced not because they wanted an end to colonial domination, but because they hoped the British or French might restore to them lands expropriated by the Germans in 1913.[17]

IV

Just when the "Kamerun idea" became an article of political currency in the Cameroons is unclear, but it is almost certain that it was not before 1948 in either territory.[18] In the

---

[17] A. Owona, op. cit. p. xii.

[18] Detailed discussion of the growth of political life in the two Cameroons maybe found in David Gardinier, *Cameroon, United Nations Challenge to French Policy* (London: Oxford University Press, 1963); Franz Ansprenger, *Politik im Schwarzen Afrika* (Cologne: Westdeutcher Verlag, 1961), Chaps. XI and XXV; Edwin Ardener, "the Political History of Cameroon," *World Today*, Vol. XVIII, No. 8 (Aug. 1962) p. 341; and in this writer's *Cameroun: From Mandate to Independence* (Los Angeles: University of California Press, 1964), and the Cameroun chapters in G. Carter (ed.), *Five African States* (Ithaca: Cornell University Press, 1963) and

French Cameroun, the several government-sponsored groups, which the French formed just prior to the outbreak of the Second World War to give young Camerounian *evolués* the opportunity to express themselves, limited themselves to voicing support for a continuation of the French mandate and requesting greater African participation in the administration of the territory. Even after the end of the war, on the heels of the creation of the trusteeship system and massive French constitutional reforms, budding nationalists found sufficient battle cries in demands for still broader political reforms and the speedy attainment of the independence promised under the Trusteeship Agreement. In 1948, however, the Union des Populations du Cameroun (UPC, formed April 10. 1948), included in its program the goal of the suppression of the "artificial boundaries" created in 1916 between the two Cameroons. In the British Cameroons, it is probable that the unification issue was first raised by the French Cameroons Welfare Union (FCWU), founded early in 1948 by R. G. K. Dibonge and a group of emigré Douala living in the British Southern Cameroons. The issue was quickly seized upon by Dr. E. M. L. Endeley, a young Southern Cameroonian physician active in the Cameroons Development Corporation Workers Union and several ethnic-based political organizations, who headed a consortium of political groups calling itself the Cameroons Federal Union.

It is important to point out that each of the three groups mentioned above adopted the "Kamerun idea" for its own particular purposes. The FCWU saw in unification a vehicle for reasserting old pan-Douala claims and securing

---

J. S. Coleman and C. Rosberg, (eds.), *Political Parties and National Integration in Tropical Africa*(Berkeley: University of California Press, 1964).

preferential economic treatment for its members; The CFU-to which the FCWU belonged-and Endeley espoused unification as an issue which might force the colonial administration into concessions on Bakweri tribal claims for land, which might create support for demands for an autonomous Southern Cameroons province within Nigeria and gain the support of the FCWU. In 1948, Endeley had little interest in unification as a realizable goal; his primary interest was to find leverage with which to gain for the Southern Cameroons a more advantageous position within Nigeria. David Gardinier, assessing Endeley's motives, contends that the publicity given Togolese demands for unification at the United Nations might also have persuaded Endeley of the potentials of this new approach. The UPC and its President, Rueben Urn Nyobe, almost certainly profited from the Togolese example. He saw that unification coupled with the goal of independence might become the leitmotif around which Cameroonian nationalist symbols could be developed. The evidence further suggests that Urn Nyobe needed an issue both popular enough to win the support of a relatively apathetic electorate and to attract the attention of the United Nations.

Without tracing the convolutions of political life in the two trust territories after 1948, it must be added that both Endeley and Urn Nyobe's initial assessments of the value of the unification issue were fully borne out by the subsequent events. By 1955 unification (now, "reunification") had become a major programmatic goal of all major political parties and groups, though with varying degrees of emphasis, in the French Cameroun. It remained one of the main goals of the Union Camerounaise, the Party which eventually led the French Cameroun to independence in 1960, and subsequently, to unification with the British Southern Cameroons.

Ironically enough, the UPC, proscribed between 1955 and 1960, did not share in the fruits of the achievement. Endeley headed the first Government of a Southern Cameroons granted quasi-federal status within Nigeria, 'though his shift away from unification with Cameroun to integration within Nigeria lost him both his Government and the credit for the unification of the two territories that resulted in 1961. The political benefits that accrued from unification went to John H. Foncha and his Kamerun National Democratic Party (KNDP), formed in 1955 to push for the unificationist goal in the face of Endeley's vacillations.

V

Every nationalist ideology contains elements of political mythology, and few political myths are more valuable than those that legitimate ideological values by providing them with traditional or historical bases.

For most African states the search for the legitimating myth has become a matter of the utmost importance. Where historical myths are available as part of a cultural tradition or had factual substance in history, they can be readily incorporated into the nationalist ideology. If this is not the case, then they must be manufactured, as in this sense the pseudo-historical "Kamerun idea" became part of the Cameroonian nationalist vocabulary. It is not claimed here that Cameroonian nationalist ideology, of which the "Kamerun idea" is a basic component, has been the only or even the most important element holding the two parts of the Cameroon federation together. Certainly the strong personalities of such Cameroon leaders as John Foncha and Ahmadou Ahidjo, the growing interdependence of the two states and the political compromises that made the federation workable have all contributed to the amalgamation.

What can be argued from the facts is that without widespread acceptance of some form of the "Kamerun idea" by Cameroonian leaders and by a substantial portion of the population in both states, the union might not have come about in the first place, or when it did, might not have lasted through its first three years. .

To summarize, four utilities and successes of the unification myth may be discerned. First, although the myth was originally conceived as a tactical weapon to further political goals other than unification, it quickly became a major item in the programs of almost all Cameroon parties and political groups.

Second, it was ideally suited as a device to focus discontent against both Britain and France for alleged sins of commission or omission. By idealizing the German period as a golden age in which the Kamerun was one, the French and British administrations could be made to look that much the worse by comparison. The accidents of history which deprived the Germans of their empire have, interestingly enough, provided them with unexpected benefits. Germany is highly well thought of in the Cameroons, and relations between the German Federal Republic and the Cameroon Federal Republic have been extremely warm and cordial.

Third, the myth provided one of the best ideological foundations for Cameroonian nationalism. "Reunification" proved sufficiently general to be understandable, sufficiently specific to seem attainable and sufficiently effective as a symbol to be appealing.

Finally, because it came upon the scene in 1948, rather than later, it had the opportunity to become part of the ideological vocabulary of both leaders and politically conscious people in the growing polities of the two states.

Rupert Emerson has perceptively pointed out that what most African states lack is the opportunity "to age in the wood," a process during which the common core of nationality grows and is nurtured to maturity.[19] Perhaps twelve years is not much time for a nationalism to grow, but the fact remains that when in 1961, the issue of unification was put to the electoral test in the British Cameroons, a large majority of voters consciously chose to implement the "Kamerun idea." As for the French Cameroun, the very fact that by 1955 almost all major political parties and groups had adopted "unification" into their programs, speaks, as least presumptively, for the widespread acceptance of the idea. It is fair to conclude that there had developed, by 1961 at least those minimal outlines of a sense of a Cameroonian community that made the federation seem both acceptable and even desirable to an important segment of the leadership and the articulate populations in both states.

VI

It would, of course, be foolish to generalize for all recent cases of partition and unification in Africa on the basis of the single example of the Cameroons. That example does, however, permit some pointed questions to be raised about other successful or unsuccessful territorial amalgamations on the continent. What elements of cohesion were lacking, for example, in the Union of African States, the Mali Federation, and the Central African Federation? The available literature

---

[19] Rupert Emerson, "National-Building in Africa," in K. W. Deutsch and W. Foltz (eds.), Nation Building (New York: Atherton Press, 1963) pp. 104-108 passim.

on these spectacular failures reveals at least that all three lacked that general acceptance and understanding by leadership and populations that might have made them workable. All three lacked, in short, trans-territorial nationalism of the most rudimentary sort.

In the case of Mali, it appears that the founders of the union-Leopold Senghor of Senegal, Modibo Keita of the Soudan, and Hubert Maga of Dahomey-must have overestimated the sense of community that developed out of their states' participation in the French West African Federation and their own common political experiences. And perhaps most importantly of all, a Malian nationalist ideology had neither been developed by the Federation's leaders nor embodied beyond the most superficial references to the bygone glories of the medieval African empire of Mali.

The case of the Union of African States was not much different, since the only thing that held the quasi-federation together was the personal ties between Nkrumah, Sekou Toure and Modibo Keita, plus a vague common ideology that remained vague precisely because the three leaders were more concerned with developing viable ideological bases for their own particular states than for the union as a whole. And of course, the difference in ideological language was exacerbated by an actual language barrier posed by the fact that the Ghanaian elite would only communicate effectively in English, while the elite in Mali and Guinea would speak only French.

Finally, it seems astounding today to think that anyone in 1953 could have been optimistic about the future of the Central African Federation. It is now clear that the basic cement which kept it together was composed of the racial ties of its white settlers; a bond unable to withstand the pressures of a black majority denied a voice in the creation of the

Federation and unwilling to accept an unequal "partnership" as the basis for its continuation. For all the good intentions lavished upon it, the Central African Federation was built without the sense of community it needed to survive.

In none of these three essays at political union was there an attempt to lay an ideological foundation of sufficient strength. Perhaps the lack of a traditional-historical mythology proved crucial in all three cases.

Chapter 3

An Ambassadorial Briefing, 1980

Cameroon remained Le Vine's major African focus throughout the 1960s, but career transitions were under way by 1970. Once settled at Washington University in St. Louis, only a brief visit back in 1965 and another during his appointment in the political science department, University of Ghana (Legon), 1969-1971, augmented his direct Cameroon experience so as to guide the 1971 book. But the Ghana sojourn, as for his colleague there from Israel, Naomi Chazan, contributed new scholarly perspectives and dimensions. Nkrumah's fall and its grim aftermath in Ghana located Le Vine in a crisis zone of greater magnitude than Cameroon's, and his publications from that point forward registered emerging interests in corruption, militarism and security, and in a more comparative study of Africa. His one major Cameroon publication during the 1970s was a collaboration with his doctoral student Roger Nye on *Historical Dictionary of Cameroon* (1974), inaugurating a series of comprehensive nation-by-nation guides to Africa originally edited by Jon Woronoff for Scarecrow Press that continues to appear forty years later, with the same format and with updates as well as new country volumes (Le Vine's 1974 dedication is of interest, recognizing "the memory of Harry Rudin, who set the standard of Cameroon historical scholarship"). His own writings and Nathalie's memory indicate that Victor's 1970s travels there were infrequent and brief, limited to lectures under United States Information Agency or similar auspices.

His virtual absence "on the ground" in Cameroon between 1971 and a University of Yaounde 1981-1982 Fulbright Fellowship appointment by no means removed Le Vine from academic and wider circles where his country expertise came into play. His 2006 *curriculum vitae* cites "1971-present: Consultant to U.S. Peace Corps, USIA, State and Defense Departments" and his next writing offered here, drawn from his unpublished archival materials, surely at the time meant for "limited circulation" rather than the public, demonstrates his continued immersion in Cameroon studies and the wider spectrum of his interests and expertise the 1970s provided. This was an 11 June 1980 U.S. State Department "Briefing for Ambassador-Designate Hume Horan." It gave Le Vine the opportunity to frame Cameroon's condition and significance for a directly engaged diplomat taking on his first ambassadorial post. The text described what was still a nation-building work in progress in its variety of strategic settings, surveyed the delicate balance of forces on issues as crucial as the presidential succession to Ahidjo, and reached an appropriately open-ended "whither Cameroon?" assessment. One interesting turn of phrase cited Victor Hugo to brief Horan on the need to concern himself with "the tree seen from the perspective of its roots," followed immediately by Le Vine's own comment that "Cameroon's problems become much more visible" in that light. Another passage used the vocabulary of a younger scholar of Cameroon and anticipated other newcomers to the field, when Le Vine quoted Jean-François Bayart's recent "Bonapartist" state usage for Cameroon (1978), a reference quickly joined in the literature by Richard Joseph's "Gaullist" characterization (1979, not used here, although Le Vine surely knew of it), and then reprised as "Vichist" in the Yaounde version I heard (1995) within the next generation's dissident intellectual circles.

This text, Le Vine's free- and far-ranging mid-career Cameroon survey, included particularly useful citations to other scholars' views as well as appendices about the anatomy of current politics and politicians. It was couched in language simultaneously so informal, intimate, nuanced and stylish that an editor is (I think) wisest to leave it to readers both to enjoy (as I did) their access to an originally "private distribution" text and to judge for themselves what was conveyed in this "inner U.S. policy circle" document covering (in more current usage than Le Vine's) "all the options" for assessing, ca. 1980, Cameroon's past, present and future.

[illegible] Liberia (2008) [illegible] the next generation [illegible]

[illegible]

This [illegible] [illegible] and [illegible] [illegible] useful [illegible]

[illegible]

[illegible]

Briefing for Ambassador-Designate Hume Horan, at the Department of State, Washington, D.C., June 11, 1980

This may be a good time to assess both the political distance Cameroon has come since 1960, when the (then) Republic of Cameroon became independent, and the distance it must still travel to achieve the regime's self-proclaimed goals of national unity, social integration, and political mobilization. Twenty years is not a very long time in the history of most countries; in Africa, however, where it almost seems that time has been compressed by an extraordinary melee of spectacular national events, twenty years is like a century. This relates to one of the main reasons why Cameroon commands our attention: it is one of the very few African countries to emerge from the first twenty years of independence with a healthy economy, and a polity still unscarred by the all too common traumas afflicting its neighbors-civil war, coups d'état, military dictatorship, brutal tyranny. And it has done so, even more remarkably, with its early leadership core still relatively intact.

This is not to say that Cameroon's first twenty years have been untroubled, or that there are not strains, even tears in the political fabric of the country. It is worth pointing out, moreover, that the skeptics – professional and amateur - have not been silent; I think all of us, at some point (or persistently) have voiced doubts about the ability of the Cameroonian political edifice to remain standing. I fear that I've been doing so since 1960; the UPC did so much earlier, and its friends and latter-day sympathizers still do so with unabated zeal. Yet, despite all predictions and early death-notices, the system has survived, and survived to confound us all.

Perhaps in our political assessment we might pay some attention to the fact of Cameroon's survival - however unfashionable or hurtful to our egos the exercise might be. That done, we are also obliged to ask if we are not somehow deluding ourselves; whether the picture of Cameroonian stability and progress we see today is not the product of our own wishful thinking. There is an obverse to the picture, and even the most sympathetic of observers have been obliged upon closer examination to wonder if the vices of Cameroon's virtues may not ultimately overwhelm her. Does Cameroon's stability as (J.F.Médard suggests) rest on an all-too fragile base? Is its "union based on disunity "? [20]

First, then, (rather than describing the most recent events in Cameroon) let me speak to some of the more conspicuous of the factors contributing directly to Cameroon's survival (and, perhaps, to its stability as well).

1. Luck. It may be very unscientific, but I very strongly suspect that part of the reason for Cameroon's stability is the fact that most of its revolution - its baptism of civil violence - was over before it became independent. However one feels about the UPC, the failure of its revolt - or the success of its calculated suppression, if you agree with Professor Joseph - helped to make Cameroonians more amenable to the regime's authority. The revolt (or suppression) was as bloody as any such incident elsewhere; but I have no doubt that it helped to create what Willard Johnson called an "integrative backlash." Philippe Decraene, who has been watching Cameroon longer than any of us, put it well: "It is indispensable to look to the

---

[20] J.-F. Médard, "L'Etat sous-developpé au Cameroun," in Année Africaine 1977 (Paris: A Pedone, 1979), pp. 35-84.

1960's for an explanation of why a pall of sullenness and depression weighs on Cameroon politics."[21] Cameroonians have also been eyewitness to the political upheavals of their neighbors--and to the attendant barbarities. Some 40-50,000 refugees from the Nigerian civil war, perhaps 45,000 from Equatorial Guinea/Rio Muni, another 40-50,000 from Chad, several thousand from the CAR, have all been forceful reminders that however much Cameroonians might resent their regime, it was and is comparatively less brutal, and it has managed to keep the internal Cameroonian peace. (Those who, in 1960-61, had advocated integration with Nigeria had a good reason, a few years later, to be grateful that they had lost the referendum. However uncomfortable the union with the francophone East, it was still better than getting involved in the Biafran secession.)

2. Leadership. J.F. Bayart argues that Ahidjo has constructed a "Bonapartist" state,[22] and indeed, his autocratic rule has been vigorously castigated by both old enemies (such as Abel Eyinga) and contemporary Cameroonian intellectuals. However one describes his rule, it is unquestionably autocratic - the regime (still) revolves around Ahidjo, and he makes all the ultimate and vital decisions. I have no illusions on the subject: Ahidjo is no democrat, and Cameroon is no democracy. The regime probably holds (a good many)

---

[21] Philippe Decraene, "Cameroon: Ahmadou Ahidjo's quest for unity," The Guardian, Feb. 25, 1979, p. 12. (Translation from Le Monde, February 6, 7, 1979).

[22] In particular, see his "Regime de parti unique et systèmes d'inégalité et de domination au Cameroun: esquisse," *Cahiers d'Etudes Africaines* 69-70: XVIII (1978), pp. 6-35.

political prisoners, and they are not well-treated.[23] Elections, such as they are, are "non-competitive," tending to be occasions for ritual affirmations of loyalty and political display. Yet Ahidjo has shown some highly pragmatic moves: (a) the cooptation of many of his political enemies in the 1960's; (b) the experiment with Federation, as much a calculated if temporary concession to the West Cameroon leadership as anything else; (c) the judicious care he has taken to select a mix of politicians and technicians in his various cabinets, including the rather intelligent balancing of regional and ethnic interests in the government and the Party (UNC). He may in fact control the system through some sort of "northern Mafia"; but the composition of his governments and party central committees belies that charge. Decraene (in 1979) cites a Cameroon bank president on this point as it applies to Cameroonian banking: "It's a northerner who runs the Banque Industrielle et Commerciale du Cameroun, a man from the Coast at the head of the Société Camerounaise des Banques, while the heads of the Banque Internationale pour l'Afrique Occidentale, the Société Générale des Banques and the Cameroon Bank are from the south central, western, and English-speaking regions of the country, respectively."[24] In any case, the governmental leadership, though it contains a number of important "fidèles de la révolution," tends to be a judicious mix of ages, skills (with technical expertise and education in the majority), ethnic background and regional representation. A cursory look at the Government he named in November, 1979, only confirms the point. It is, in most respects, a balanced group combining old and young, North

---

[23] Amnesty International's estimate in 1979 was 200 political prisoners. Torture and other grave violations of human rights were also alleged.

[24] Decraene, "Cameroon ...," p. 12.

and South, East and West, in a stable amalgam. (See Annexes A and B for details.)

The top leadership in the party is, of course, a different story: the "vieux turbans" predominate (certainly in the Central Committee – though less so in the functional commissions). But note: the party, for all its hegemonial and formal powers, has also become a sort of prebendiary pasture. At last glance, I noted at least eight – perhaps ten - people who were in the UNC central committee despite the fact that they were semi- retired and/or little active in party or official life: (the late) Andre Fouda, John Foncha, (the elder) Tchoungui, Moussa Yaya, Dr. E. Endeley, Prince Rene Douala Bell, Bernard Fonlon, G. Garba, Jean Ekwabi, etc. (The National Assembly also contains many such people.)

What all this means is that even though Ahidjo pretty much has the final say in all important matters (in particular the armed forces and defense, foreign policy, internal security), he has taken care to see that the day-to-day running of affairs are in relatively competent – and loyal – hands. He plays, and plays well, what Médard calls "la politique de l'équilibre."

Also to Ahidjo's credit is the fact that he has avoided the excesses of a full-blown personality cult. They have a way of backfiring on their subjects. There is, to be sure, a sort of mini-cult, complete with the standard portrait – pagnes, griots officiels, adulatory biographies, pictures everywhere, and praise-singing - yet, given his personality, he remains relatively low keyed, and whatever charisma now surrounds him tends to be institutionalized. Nor has he indulged in the massive and conspicuous accumulation of wealth of some of his peers. There is corruption but it seems to have been kept at tolerable levels. I must add that he has not been reluctant to "talk turkey" to his people, and denounce corruption and inefficiency, as witness his speech at the recent Bafoussam party congress. As "father of the country," he is certainly privileged to deliver the occasional pointed homily. What is more important, people do listen to him and his words, which while they may not reform the sinful or inspire the lazy, are taken very seriously. If he has anything, he has gravitas in the classical sense of a command presence. The respect he commands and the fact of firm control has also enabled him to wait out the traditional chiefs and ensure the succession of his loyalists to those positions, as well as periodically "recirculate" his advisors to the best effect.

In sum, he has managed to stay on top by being smarter than his opponents, and by careful manipulation of the levers of institutional power. He giveth and he taketh away, and he does so with equal intelligence. Even more significant, I think, is that he has also shown no hesitation to display official repression (when he thinks it's needed), but has carefully kept it both infrequent and below levels that would incite widespread hatred and subversive opposition. I don't know if there is some sort of threshold for violent opposition; but Ahidjo's regime seems to have been able to get away with the periodic act of brutal repression, at least until now.

3. Economic good health. I suspect that one of the reasons why Cameroonians generally – for all their sullenness—have been willing to put up with the nastier aspects of the regime, and indeed to show support when it is called for, is the fact that the regime has managed to deliver the economic goods. This outcome may also be partly a matter of good luck (2 m. metric tons of oil p.a. is certainly

good luck[25]), but it is also due to intelligent management. (Note that other, comparatively rich African countries have gone down to near-economic disaster as much because of mis-management as anything else; Ghana is a prime example and so is Congo/Brazzaville.) I do not doubt the regime could do much better, - in particular for its Anglophone citizens, whose restlessness is probably caused in part by considerable disappointment over the substantive economic payoffs of "unity." Perhaps, again, there's an element of luck. Cameroon is not a single-crop economy; it did not suffer as much from the widespread fluctuations of the cocoa and coffee markets of the early 70's as did other African states. It has managed to diversify its markets, it was not victimized too much by the great droughts, and it was and is able to attract substantial development capital and foreign assistance (very much a function of its relative stability), and of course, it did find oil in exploitable amounts just when the economy began to slide under the impact of the world-wide post-1973

[25] Assuming the standard conversion factor of 7.3 barrels per metric ton, production of 2 million barrels per annum (to which Ahidjo admitted at Bafoussam), comes to 40,000 barrels per day (bpd). Reliable informants in the oil companies now privately say production is closer to 60,000 bpd, which comes to ca. 3 million tons per annum. In 1979 exports of Cameroon crude brought in an estimated $200 million, but products imports (petroleum and distillates) cost ca. $106 million. When the Victoria refinery comes on line (possibly before the end of 1980), and assuming its initial production will be devoted principally to cover current Cameroonian needs (ca. 26,000-28,000 bpd), that would leave ca. 30,000 bpd for export. At a posted price somewhere around the current wobbly OPEC floor, 1981 could bring Cameroon ca. $350 million on her oil transactions alone. And if the offshore finds near Kribi do in fact yield substantial and exploitable LNG returns, the picture looks even brighter.

balance of payments-capital drain crisis. Oil can cushion a lot of shocks, though it is not (as I suggest later) necessarily an unmixed political blessing.

As I said earlier, I would not be true to my calling if I did not also point out the system's vulnerabilities. I will not announce its imminent collapse – though the unexpected is always possible, witness Liberia. Thus far, what has been described is the system, writ large. It appears solid, well-entrenched, its prospects favorable. Yet, seen from below – as Victor Hugo put it, "the tree seen from the perspective of its roots" - Cameroon's problems become much more visible, and the system begins to look much less solid than (it did) at first glance.

Certainly, recent events and developments in Cameroon entitle us to ask, as did Médard, whether the solidity of the regime, its alleged stability, is no more than a carefully contrived facade.[26] The Dollé incident, the deaths at Douga, student unrest in Yaounde, the abortive subalterns' coup of 1979, the strikes of 1977 and 1979, increasing corruption at all levels of government, the increased willingness of Anglophones to express their resentments openly, may all well be symptoms of some underlying problems which the regime has either not addressed, or neglected, or for which it has been unable to find appropriate answers. The negative side of the ledger, then, must at least contain entries for the following:

1. Leadership and the Succession. Ahidjo is 56, comparatively young for an African leader in power twenty-two years. He is a member of a very exclusive club: African heads of state and government in power since the

---

[26] Médard, "L'Etat sous-developpé au Cameroun ," pp. 55-5.

independence decades of 1957-1968. Membership in the "founding fathers' club" had, however, declined rapidly during the past several years, and, in addition to Ahidjo, there are now only Senghor, Sékou Touré, Houphouet Boigny, Nyerere, Hastings Banda, Seretse Khama, Kenneth Kaunda, King Sobhuza, and Daouda Jawara left in Sub-Saharan Africa.[27] The problem, it need hardly be pointed out, lies both in Ahidjo's political longevity, and in the fact that in the process of remaining in office for so long and consolidating power in his own hands, he has effectively created the myth of his own indispensability. "Qui autre?" He has not groomed a successor, and whenever he hints that he may not stand (again) for re-election to the Presidency, the comparison between him and his potential replacements makes him look all the more indispensable and he (again) agrees to succeed himself "for the good of the country." I think this ritual may once have been a charade; it is probably real now, since to all intents and purposes, there is no one who can effectively replace him so long as he is alive and able to function. To be sure, the recent constitutional change makes the Prime Minister the President's successor should the latter die or be unable to perform the duties of his office. In practical terms, should (for example) Ahidjo pass suddenly from the scene while Biya is still Prime Minister, it will take an extraordinary act of collective self-discipline at the top of the Cameroonian leadership heap to prevent a damaging - and possibly violent - fight for the succession. There is no lack of able people at the top, and it is not impossible that the succession can and will

[27] Excluding the Arab north, where Bourguiba still clings to power, and Angola, Mozambique, Guinea Bissau, Cape Verde, Sao Tome and Principe, Djibouti, and the Comoros, all of which became independent during the 1970's.

be arranged peacefully (witness the Kenyatta-Arap Moi, Mba-Bongo, Tubman-Tolbert transfers), but given the relative scarcity of such events, one is not inclined to be overly sanguine. Happily, Ahidjo is still healthy and able, and will thus undoubtedly be able to serve out his next term of office. Yet, the longer he remains in office, the longer the odds against him, and unless he begins now to help prepare for an orderly succession, the odds will get even longer. (Recall that there is not even a Vice-President at present. At one time the prospect of an Anglophone President may have been sufficient reason to eliminate the position; that danger seems less frightening now.)

2. "L'Etat Mou." Jean-François Médard devotes considerable effort to making the point that whatever national integration has been achieved in Cameroon, it has been achieved at the top: "integration étatique," not national. The state, says Médard, is a shell, and it will remain fragile so long as national authority does not also translate into effective local authority and stable mass political loyalty. Bureaucratic corruption, official incompetence, the absence of conscience professionelle among government officials, and a widespread lack of respect for law and authority, all tend to undermine the attempts of the regime to promote national unity and social integration. At the top, the state is visible and vigorous; at the bottom it is, at best inefficient, as worst, "mou," or spineless.[28] These are, perhaps, exaggerations, but there is certainly sufficient evidence of some erosion of the regime's legitimacy. If the regime can keep discontent at manageable levels; if it can successfully continue to co-opt, seduce, pay off, or quietly silence its potential challengers; if it can continue to provide visible and reasonably fair distribution of

---

[28] Médard, op. cit.

economic and political goods, it may not run into trouble from below, or from opportunists within the establishment. Thus far, it has managed to survive, and for some of the reasons noted above. Yet there are also some signs of ossification, perhaps even petrification in the system. The party, it now appears, exists primarily to occupy as much of the political terrain as possible, principally to inhibit the growth of organized opposition. At the local level the party is all too often simply a device to ensure regular extraction of party dues, and to bring out the people for the periodic political rituals decreed from Yaounde - elections, national holidays, and the like. It has not, apparently, been effective for some time in mobilizing people for the tasks of "national construction," and the grand slogans from the top fall, more often than not, on deaf ears. And if the party superstructure remains the prebendiary pasture it has become, the party as a whole will crystallize even further.

3. Oil as a political explosive. The regime has been wise, I think, to play down possibilities inherent in the country's recent petroleum good fortune. The fact remains, however, that the government's very efforts to minimize the role of oil in the economy (by emphasizing the agricultural developments, by being vague about production and new finds) have helped fuel wild and exaggerated rumors about the size, potential and value of the offshore deposits[29]. It is

---

[29] A paragraph in a recent article in Jeune Afrique (no. 1002, 19 March 1980, p. 81) is to the point, despite its condescending tone:

Mais, sagesse ou coquetterie, les dirigeants souhaitent qu'on ne parle pas de l'avenir pétrolier de leur pays. Et lorsqu'on insiste pour savoir le raison de cette discrétion, c'est peine si certains d'entre eux consentent vous confier sur le ton de la confidence: "C'est pour ne pas tourner la tête à nos compatriotes et leur donner la tentation d'abandonner l'agriculture

not improbable that the fact that the oil fields are offshore to (Anglophone) Fako Division may have helped fan some banked Anglophone separatist flames. To older but persistent complaints that Anglophone Cameroonians were never given their due as partners in the old federation,[30] may now have been added fears that the Anglophones will not get fair benefit from the oil bonanza. Add to this the problem of keeping expectations down, and the difficulties of dealing with the economics of an oil boom, if such in fact occurs, and the mixture becomes potentially explosive.

How far, then, has Cameroon come on the road to national unity, social integration, and political - and economic - mobilization? Remarkably far, if only by the measures of survival, relative political stability, and economic progress. Given the extraordinary socio-ethnic diversity of the country, and the facts of its political history, unification and integration from the top down may have been the only strategy that could work. Yet, the task is incomplete, and there is the real possibility that the architects of the strategy may lose the initiative that has been theirs since 1960. Cameroon's leaders may be racing against time now, and one

---

qui doit demeurer la priorité de nos priorités." La défiance des autorités à l' endroit du dieu pétrole est telle que les revenues de l'or noir accumulés depuis 1978 (début de l'exploitation), et qui représenteraient déjà plus de 50 milliards de CFA (1miliard de FF), n'ont, pas êtes injectes dans les circuits économiques. Ils ont bloqués dans un compte bancaire à l'étranger ou ils "font des petits" sans menacer l'équilibre interne du troupeau.

[30] See Jacques Benjamin's Les Camerounais occidentaux (Montréal: Presses Universitaires de Montréal, 1972), which I understand is still proscribed in Cameroon.

can only wish them flexibility, wisdom, and more good luck in the next few years.

Appendix A: Key Background Data on Cameroonian Cabinet Officers

Appendix A: Key Background Data on Cameroonian Cabinet Officers.

Country: CAMEROON
Source and Date of Info.: Afr. Res. Bulletin – PSC Series; 11/21/79 [illegible]
Effective date: 11/18/79

No. posts: 24
(does not include all Junior ministers)

Name of Minister	Provenance	Age 1980	Posit. Age*	Education	Profession or Occupation
Biya, Paul	South Center	47	1968 12	H (licence, DES, diplôme)	Civil serv.
Daoudou, Sadou	North	54	1960 20	S	• •
Kwayeb-Kotte, Enoch	South west	56	1959 21	H (license, Law)	Lawyer/Magistrate
Ayissi Mvodo, Victor	South	47	1969 11	" • •	" "
Egbe Tabi, Emmanuel	West	53	1961 19	" (BA)	Civil serv.
Doumba, Joseph-Chas.	North	45	1974 6	" (license, Law)	" " (& lawyer)
Onana Awana, Charles	South Center	57	1960 20	" " "	Economist & civil serv.
Keutcha, Jean	South west	57	1964 16	S (Agric. H.S.)	Civ. serv. (& agric. technician)
Daouda, Youssoufa	North	38	1972 8	H (Agric., Paris)	" " (& agric. engineer)
Ndam, Njoya	West Center	38	1975 5	H (license, Law)	" "
Fokam Kamga, Paul	South	50	1967 13	" " "	• "
Ayang, Luc	South	?	1977 3	"	" "
Tonye Mbog, Félix	South West	46	1972 8	" " "	" "
Mayimbone Nlong, Gilbert	South west	?	1977 3	" (ENAM)	" "
Andze Tchoungui, Gilbert	South Central	50	1975 5	S	• "
Maikano, Abdoulaye	North	48	1975 5	H (Veterinary)	Veterinarian
Yang Yandji, Philémon	South	33	1975 5	H (licence, Law	Lawyer/Magistrate
Ze Nguelé, René	South	43	1975 5	• (• lettres)	Teacher
Songue Benga, Christian	west	56	1972 8	H (AB, U of London)	Civil serv.
Tsanga, Delphine	South Center	45	1970 10	S (Nursing)	Nurse
Dontsop, Paul	South west	43	1975 5	H (IHEOM, ENAM)	Civil serv.
Bwele, Guillaume	South Center	?	1979 0	H (Agreg., lettres)	" "
Ngome Kome, Albert	West (?)	41	1979 0	n.i.	" "
Moustapha, Ahmadou	North	35	1975 5	H (ENAM)	• "

* Positional) Age: Year of entry into cabinet, no. years in cabinet

Appendix B: Analysis of Background Factors of Cameroonian Cabinet Named November 18, 1979

1. Movement: Three out (Sengat Kuoh, Elangwe, Yondo), two new members(Bwele and Ngome Koma); total of twelve shifted .

2. Provenance: 5 (or 6) from North; 2(or 3) from West/Anglophone; 16 from South, of which 4 or 5 are clearly South Center, 5 or 6 are from South West, and the rest are Southeast and Coast.

3. Age: 8 are between 57 and 50, 6 between 45 and 49, 3 between 40 and 44, and 4 are between 33 and 39. (N: 21)

4. Positional ages: 20 are holdovers from the 1975 cabinet, 3 from the Independence Cabinet of 1960. 9 have been in the cabinet 10 years or more, and 5 have been cabinet ministers 16 or more year. Only Sadou Daoudou has held the same portfolio (Armed Forces) from the beginning; everyone else - excepting the newcomers - has been shifted around at least once (some as many as five times), and some, such as Onana Awana, have been in and out once or twice .

5. Education: 19 (of 23 on which information was available) have attended some institution of higher learning ("H"); that is 82.6% or the total. 4 have attended at least a secondary school ("S"); that is, 17.4%.

6. Occupation/Profession: This represents occupation/profession when the individual entered government service; in the case of civil servants, it is the only occupation/profession of the individual. Civil servants

account for 17 of the 24 (70.8%), Lawyers are 3/24 (12.5%), other professions are 4/24 (16.6%).

Note: As far as I can tell, this cabinet continues a long tradition of well-balanced cabinets. In particular, the Bamileke continue to well-represented despite the occasional "effervescence" of the Bamileke regions. I don 't know what Sengat Kuoh, Elangwe, and Yondo are doing now, but Ahidjo often provides a number of alternatives that enable him to bring back to the inner circle those he has cast out : "en reserve pour la Republique" (continued high salary but no official position), rustication to some local administrative position, a prebend in the Party. Unless they have done something truly offensive, those whom he does not eventually recall have generally been permitted to enter or resume profitable civilian callings.

Chapter 4

Crisis Paper I, 1984

Next come two previously unpublished writings, this chapter's dated 1984 and the next's 1992. They are sensible to bracket despite the eight year interval. Le Vine's Fulbright semester at the University of Yaounde, 1981-1982, fully reacquainted him with Cameroon. Occasional visits and the extra-curricular consulting continued to refresh his Cameroonian connections thereafter. Thus, when the 1984 coup attempt and then the 1990-1992 democratization campaign challenged what had been one of Africa's most stable governments, Le Vine recognized the urgency and produced seasoned analyses during these crisis times.

He had always (with reservations, as we have seen above and will again below) regarded Ahidjo's presidency as a skillful exercise in statecraft, and there are continual queries throughout his Cameroon writings about whether succession to the office, vested in any individual, however collectively supported, could be managed as competently and peaceably as during Ahidjo's two decades. But trouble flared after 1980 in circumstances still debated. Ahidjo retired from the presidency, 2 November 1982 but not from his leadership role in the ruling Cameroon National Union (CNU) political party apparatus he had built and sustained over a quarter century. Paul Biya, appointed Cameroon's first prime minister in 1975 and reappointed and designated as Ahidjo's successor in 1979, took the presidential oath of office 6 November 1982. Following a year and a half of their uncomfortable coexistence in state and party offices, punctuated by Ahidjo's resignation from the CNU presidency, 23 August 1983, there was a 6-7 April 1984 coup attempt by Republican Guard officers, identified as northern Ahidjo loyalists. Recall Le Vine's description of the republic's 1 January 1960 inauguration as a parallel: 1984's crisis was serious enough to claim perhaps 1,000 fatalities during the fire fights and through the purges following its failure to dislodge Biya, and to shift Cameroon from its "stable" profile into the ranks of African nations where conflict, having reached this breaking point, removed governance from an always contested but nonetheless established level of confidence and equilibrium onto more precarious terrain.

It happened that a "Cameroon Day" conference already scheduled at The Johns Hopkins University's Advanced School for International Studies (Baltimore) assembled Le Vine and 400 others 13 April 1984, within a week of the coup attempt and its apparent (but who yet knew how complete?) suppression. The venue was both geographically and strategically very close to the highest American policy circles, and Cameroon's ambassador Paul Pondi and half his embassy staff were there. It is clear that Le Vine's "Cameroon's April Revolt in Perspective" paper, dated fifteen weeks later, 31 July 1984, and published here for the first time, contained and filtered as much information from both informal and official sources as anything from such a distance could have at the time (some was available 13 April for the scholars to engage, even if Cameroon embassy officials must then have been "guarded," and more emerged later). The text lacks the immediacy of an April eyewitness account but was otherwise, given Le Vine's interlude to assess the aftermath and his stature as a ranking scholarly authority, as "timely" as any such document could be.

His first page's keynote about the conference's "dominant note…a combination of apprehension and guarded optimism about Cameroon's future" led to characteristic Le Vine language as he went on to discern the issues, appraise the forces engaged and offer something new: an evaluation of Biya as well Ahidjo, in some detail. Concluding that "predictions about how he will fare would be foolish," Le Vine kept this paper from print circulation as Cameroon faced a less certain future, with a less experienced president, as its second quarter century of nationhood approached. Readers three decades later may be prompted to apply it to current and future scenarios.

Cameroon's April Revolt in Perspective

Four months may not be enough to provide proper perspective on the April attempted coup in Cameroon, but at least, given the flood of articles, analyses, official statements, and eyewitness accounts of the event, there is enough information now to permit some tentative reflections and conclusions. There is also enough information to dispel some misconceptions, correct some reporting errors, and suggest what it is that we still do not know about the event.

One set of preliminary perspectives emerged from the "Cameroon Day" conference held in Washington, D.C. on April 13. Given the conference's unexpectedly fortuitous timing, it attracted almost 400 people, an unusually large number for what had been advertised as primarily an academic affair. Sponsored by Johns Hopkins University's School of Advanced International Affairs and organized by Professors I. William Zartman and Michael Schatzberg, the conference drew not only leading scholars of Cameroon affairs (both Cameroonian and American), but also African diplomats (including M. Paul Pondi, Cameroon's ambassador, and about half his mission), officials from various Africa-related federal agencies, business people, other scholars and students, and members of the public. Youssoufa Daouda, Cameroon's Minister of the Plan and Territorial Planning, in town for a World Bank symposium, appeared briefly to reassure us that things were under control back home and to voice his appreciation for the conference and everybody's concern and interest.

If there was dominant note struck at the conference - in both the formal and informal discussions – it was a combination of apprehension and guarded optimism about

Cameroon's future. Clearly, both the attempted coup and the scale of the violence in Yaounde had taken everyone by surprise, including both Cameroonian and outside observers. Everyone with whom I spoke voiced his dismay that the attempted coup had in fact taken place, but equally praised the regular army for rallying to Biya's defense. Perhaps here was one African military properly socialized to the norms of civilian supremacy! We agreed that this was perhaps one of the few bright aspects of what was otherwise a horrifying experience. It was Professor Willard Johnson (Massachusetts Institute of Technology) who publicly voiced the crucial cautionary questions: What obligations had Biya now incurred to military in as much as it had saved both his skin and his government? What role would it now play in Biya's regime?

Certainly, it was generally agreed, Cameroon would never be the same again, and how Biya handled the passions generated by the late events might well determine if Cameroon could continue as one of the continent's most productive and stable countries. Biya was given due credit for his efforts to downplay the resurgence of north-south antagonisms evoked both by last year's "plot" and the late coup attempt. The continued presence of important northerners in Biya's government (including, visibly, M. Daouda) was taken by Professor Ndiva Kofele-Kale (who presented an important paper on the ethnic sociology of Cameroon politics) as clear evidence of the President's conciliatory intentions. Doubts nevertheless remained whether Biya's partisans could now be restrained from demanding that excessive exemplary punishment he visited on those who had so long - in the view of many southerners – deprived them of their fair share of the national redistributive pie. We all hoped for the best.

Ex-President Ahidjo, when he figured in the conference at all, came in for sharp criticism. He was denounced for having "betrayed" the country by trying to regain power after he had peacefully ceded it, excoriated for having wished the recent coup-makers well, and blamed for his "dictatorial" and "autocratic" ways. Though no one had any but circumstantial evidence that Ahidjo was in fact behind the April 6 and 7 attempt, two Cameroonians just returned from Yaounde were convinced that even if he had not directly sanctioned the uprising, some of the leaders of the attempted coup must have thought they had his blessings on the enterprise. It was also interesting to note that the question of Ahidjo's personal finances remains open for many Cameroonians: a number of participants in the conference openly speculated about what Ahidjo had done with that part of the country's oil revenues under his direct control and for which - most important - he had not been publicly accountable. (No one had anything more than conjecture and rumor to contribute on the question, but it is certainly something about which Biya will have to satisfy his people one of these days.)

The conference could not, of course, have discussed the question of participation in the attempted coup, since information on that subject was scant at the time of the conference. Thus far we have only partial information, but enough, however, to establish some interesting details. First, there were probably no more than 1,000 people actively involved: the government claimed to have arrested 1,053 people, of which 800 were subsequently set free after investigation or acquitted after trial; some 265 mutineers are listed as missing and are presumed either dead or in flight, and another 58 rebels are listed killed during the fighting. If the official figures are anywhere near being correct, that makes about 576 active participants (not, as reported widely

1,500, or 3,000), a figure which corresponds roughly to the size of the Republican Guard itself, that is, about 450 to 500 men (about the strength of a U.S. infantry battalion). The 576 figure also includes a number of civilians (several of which were among the 46 executed) as well as some policemen and Gendarmes who had joined the rebels. The Republican Guard, it should be added for the record, was armed with infantry weapons including several (probably no more than 15) armored scout cars of the M-8 and Ferret types. It had no tanks (the Cameroon army has no tanks either), no heavy artillery, and no air support. If we assume that not everyone involved has been accounted for, a reasonably tenable figure is at most 1,000. What of the ethnic, religious, and regional origins of the rebels? While the Republican Guard was overwhelmingly Muslim and northern in origin, and while almost all of its officers were Fulani, the noncoms and troopers were heavily Shoa Arab and Toupouri, traditional tribal clients of the Fulani from the "far north" along the Logone River. (The Toupouri are a mixed bag in religious matters; originally animists, many are nominal Muslims, converting more for reasons of social advancement than out of conviction. Those in the Guard were said to fit this description.) In addition to the Guard, it appears that a number of southern Gendarmes and policemen joined the rebels, and that the civilians involved included some prominent southern officials and businessmen. Thus, while the ringleaders were northerners and Fulani, the uprising was not, as Defense Minister Tsoungui claimed "99.9% northern," or Muslim in persuasion. Moreover, despite Simon Malley's assertion that two Moroccan planes landed equipment and men at Garoua, and that members of Libya's Islamic Legion had disembarked at Maroua (AfricAsia #6, June 1984), no evidence has yet been produced to substantiate either claim. And the two planes that landed in Nigeria allegedly carrying French mercenaries destined for Yaounde turned out to contain French officers on a completely innocent official training mission.

Was Ahidjo in on the attempted coup? Possibly, though evidence of direct links with the rebels has yet to be produced. It is not improbable, at the very least that the leaders of the April rebellion may have had his blessings, or thought they had. At any event, there appears to be enough evidence to suggest that the attempt had been planned well in advance and that it was Biya 's order (on April 5) to disband the Guard and reassign its elements to the north that - quite possibly, prematurely – triggered the action. (A weak case could he made for a spontaneous mutiny, given the awkwardness with which several of the main objectives, especially the airport, were attacked and taken by the rebels. The main roads from the Guard's Obili Barracks and in town are relatively well paved, and at 3:00AM, without the hindrance of traffic, the Army HQ is less than 10 minutes away. It is the involvement of civilians that gives credence to the hypothesis of a planned coup.) According to some reports Ahidjo had sought, and obtained support for a putsch from Morocco's King Haassan and Libya's Col. Kadafy: Ahidjo is also rumored to have met clandestinely with various plotters, and allegedly obtained a "hands-off" promise from the French, if not a commitment to assist him if and when he mounted his coup. Unless convincing evidence emerges which supports these reports, they remain fanciful at best; Ahidjo may have been indirectly involved, but in the absence of credible proof even that remains rumor, not fact. What is certain is that if Ahidjo himself had not sought to regain power by questionable means in 1983, his partisans would not have tried to seize it in 1984. I have no doubt that if they had been successful, Ahidjo would not have refused an invitation to return to power. At the very least, Ahidjo bears responsibility for opening the door to military intervention, a door notoriously difficult to close thereafter.

Most open to controversy is the question of causes. The proximate cause of the coup attempt, to be sure, was Biya's order to disband the Guard and redeploy its members. Beyond that, the explanations vary a good deal. The most common theme in the explanations focusses on Cameroon's "ruling class," particularly the so-called political and commercial "barons" who had gained power, privilege, and wealth through their association with Ahidjo and his regime. These people included Ahidjo's fideles in the government and bureaucracy, directors of parastatals, businessmen and industrialists become rich through government preferment, members of various legislative and advisory bodies, and the like. Though northerners and Muslims tended to be among the most visible in this group, they included people of all religious persuasions and from all regions of the country. The argument is that this group was most threatened by Biya's accession to power; his reformist and liberalizing policies had put its privileges and power in extreme jeopardy, and it was prepared to do what was necessary to defend itself. Consequently, the "barons" first persuaded Ahidjo to try to regain power by declaring the single party (over which Ahidjo continued to preside immediately after his resignation) supreme over the President and the government. Failing that, they then generated the so-called "August plot," and were again thwarted, this time with disastrous results. A military putsch then appeared the best chance of success - thus, April 6 and 7.

This argument has much to recommend it, since it does identify the group with (potentially) the most to lose under a

Biya regime, as well as those who were apparently involved in trying to topple Biya. Yet the argument is flawed for two main reasons: it fails to give due weight to Ahidjo and his role in Cameroonian events since he resigned the presidency, and fails to take into consideration both Biya's attempt to coopt many of the "barons" into his new order, and the fact that most members of the "ruling class" accepted (or reluctantly acquiesced in) the Biya succession and all that it might entail for them.

A fair reading of Ahidjo's statements and public acts during the five years preceding his resignation makes it difficult to avoid the conclusion that Ahidjo had carefully prepared his retirement, and that he left when his health, stamina, and interest could no longer warrant continuation in office. It is difficult to credit the frequent suggestion that Ahidjo reluctantly resigned because of poor health, that he made a "deal" with Biya to cede only the trappings of power, remaining on the scene as the latter's eminence grise. (For anyone who knows Ahidjo, or has watched him since 1958 - as has this writer – such an arrangement seems totally uncharacteristic of the man.) Once out of office, however, and for whatever reasons (better health, the shock of the event itself, pressure from his closest "baronial" friends and colleagues, Biya's quick popularity, or perhaps, mental instability), he apparently did change his mind about surrendering power, and put in motion the several attempts to regain it. It may well be that the "barons" were always terribly unhappy about the change, but it should he recalled that initially Ahidjo was even willing to visit exemplary punishment upon one of his closest friends and associates, Moussa Yaya, for publicly voicing displeasure about the transition. Eventually, the "barons" may have persuaded him, but the point is that he was the critical factor in their behavior; without his initiative and support not one would have dared to seek Biya's downfall.

Then too, the record shows Biya's willingness to work with Ahidjo's "barons," giving many of them the benefit of any doubts about their loyalty by keeping them in key official positions. Note, for example, that it was not until June 18, 1983 almost eight months after Ahidjo's resignation, that Sadou Naoudou, Victor Ayissi Mvodo, Samuel Eboua, and Guillaume Bwele, all Ahidjo's fideles, were finally dropped from the government, and then only when Ahidjo's opposition to Biya had become clear and open. Still other "barons" declared their support for Biya, and have remained in top positions: among others, Anglophones Solomon Tandeng Muna and Emmanuel Egbe Tabi; Joseph Charles Doumba, Bouba Bello Maigari, and Nji Yakoubou. Even the most faithful of Ahidjo's faithful, Sadou Daoudou, now without a government post, still remains a member of the Central Committee of the ruling Cameroon National Union party. The point that needs to be made is that only a part of the group of "barons" in fact made common cause with Ahidjo; very few of them were actually involved in the "August plot" and probably fewer still in the April 6 and 7 revolt. It may be that the number of active Ahidjo partisans among the "barons" is much larger than hitherto revealed, but if so, they are keeping very quiet, or they have since rallied to Biya, or their numbers are much smaller. In fact Biya is still in power, and after having successfully weathered the worst that Ahidjo and his partisans could unleash against him. That fact alone should by now have persuaded any remaining hesitant "barons" to go along with him.

What now remains are the questions posed earlier . After a plot, an attempted military coup, the execution (thus far) of forty-six people, and amidst considerable general political unease, Biya must now attempt to restore confidence in himself, his government, and the liberalizing promise of his presidency. And perhaps most crucially, he must seek a modus vivendi with the one group who most profited from the April revolt and to whom he owes a practically unpayable debt: his loyal military officers. At this point, predictions about how he will fare would be foolish; we can only hope he will succeed in calming what is still a very nervous and troubled situation.

Chapter 5

Crisis Paper II, 1992

An opportunity for crisis analysis similar to 1984's registered in the next unpublished Le Vine archival text selected for inclusion here. Like the 1984 text, 1992's had a four month gestation period. To interject the editor's related experience here (since I heard oral versions of this paper twice in 1992 after spending much of 1991 in Cameroon), I knew of its inception as Le Vine's working manuscript for a late July 1992 U.S. State Department forum in Washington (D.C.) bringing scholars of Cameroon together with Americans in strategic policy posts. We both participated in a simulation exercise for officials, some civilians, others military, charged with understanding Cameroon's second major post-independence crisis. Le Vine simulated Paul Biya's presidential role in various scenarios, I simulated John Fru Ndi's as his challenger in the election scheduled for ten weeks thereafter, 11 October. Fru Ndi had emerged in 1990 in the aging John Ngu Foncha's place, having become both Cameroon's dominant anglophone activist as chairman of a new political party, the Social Democratic Front (SDF), and the leader of a far broader coalition of opposition forces in a democratization campaign that now, two years after its launch, was increasingly though not entirely national in scope. Legislative elections earlier in 1992 had dropped Biya's Cameroon Peoples Democratic Movement (CPDM) from a virtual monopoly to a narrow plurality's hold on National Assembly seats, a stunning political landscape change. Ahidjo had reined in Foncha and other anglophones for twenty years: it was not so as Biya faced Fru Ndi, 1990-1992.

October's presidential election, which the July State Department session was designed to anticipate, would soon match these two as the chief contenders for the presidency.

Le Vine's 1992's text was not the product of a crisis as profound as 1984's, but the challenge to Biya and the CPDM, successors to Ahidjo and the CNU, was substantial. Fuller coverage of the 1990-1992 conflict is readily available elsewhere; the most relevant context to establish here, beyond the SDF's and its coalition's mobilization during those two years, is Foncha's very public, very angry mid-1990 letter of resignation from the CPDM's central committee, just as Biya's governance was being challenged on many fronts. Foncha cited reasons rehearsed three decades earlier in Le Vine's 8 April 1961 text and the introduction to it offered in Chapter 1 above; Foncha would subsequently lead a 1995 Southern Cameroons National Council (SCNC) delegation to the United Nations, moving past the SDF's advocacy for the return to a reinforced federal constitution by urging the U.N. to resume responsibilities it had vacated in 1960-1961 and to pave the way for anglophone secession from (the phrase it still insists on two decades later, pointing out the linguistic cleavage in politics) "la république."

This 1992 Le Vine text added details as it developed from July until I heard its oral delivery to a "Succession in Africa" panel at the 23-26 November 1992 African Studies Association meeting in Seattle. Le Vine meant "Succession" in both the broadly political and specifically presidential senses; the paper should be regarded as a provisional "working" document, constantly revised and not fully edited, for its original form was unpaginated and a few details were rendered incorrectly. It factored in fresh and crucial July-November "on the ground" data: the 11 October presidential election with its disputed result Cameroon's supreme court ratified in Biya's favor, and the last week of October's declaration of a state of emergency in Fru Ndi's North West Province and Fru Ndi's house arrest. By the time of the paper's Seattle presentation, it carried a far harsher appraisal of Biya than Le Vine ever wrote for Ahidjo, in line with the almost contemptuous verbal turns of phrase for Biya the editor recalls Le Vine using at both the July State Department session and the November panel.

A more nuanced and theoretical framework than in Le Vine's earlier Cameroon writing is the last feature to note before this text's reproduction. African politics scholarship was by the 1980s approaching the entire continent through a range of social science epistemology and literature the pioneer narratives lacked, especially for the analyses of political leadership and of class structures as African rulers' domination over their domestic populations intensified. New forms of scrutiny developed, country by country. Was leadership vested in a shifting elite or a permanent political class? Could its dominance be sustained? Or would challenges to autocratic governance develop? If so, on what grounds of resistance, and with what chance of success? Hence, Le Vine's references here to Antonio Gramsci, and a coverage that extended beyond the substance of governance and use of power at the state's core into ceremonial trappings, groomed publicity and intricate patronage, new to at least his Cameroonian writings, although already visible as his writings on other countries became more varied and comparative after 1970.

This new strain joined two previously established patterns in his scholarship. One is the high, perhaps unusual interest, even among political scientists, in addressing the normative and aspirational as well as practical dimensions of political and constitutional analysis, likely reflecting Le Vine's abiding concern, understandable as a part of his own experience, for the fundamental issue of what defines and differentiates citizens and subjects. The other is a conventional historian's regard for personal agency and motivation as explanatory forces in human events, revealed in the narratives about individuals all his writings sustain, and which the emphases on Ahidjo's and Biya's characters and courses of action and reaction exemplify here, however much theory and structural analysis shaped all of Le Vine's Cameroon writings.

The cumulative events Le Vine surveyed in 1992 brought the condition of Cameroon's constitutional evolution and the generic nature of the polity Ahidjo had developed during his two decades as president, and had transferred to Biya so contentiously, into serious question once again. Ten years after Ahidjo's retirement (and three years after his death in exile), Le Vine recorded the country's major early 1990s upheaval in a way that led him to this text's striking last eleven words: "the next succession in Cameroon may well be a democratic one."

Crisis and Democratic Succession in Cameroon

Presented to the panel on "Succession in Africa" at the Annual Meeting of the African Studies Association, Seattle, Washington, November 20-23, 1992

On October 11, 1992, Cameroon's voters went to the polls to elect a new President. The election, called by President Biya under pressure from the country's opposition, was to have been the first freely contested multiparty presidential election in the country's history. The periodic mandates given the first president, Ahmadou Ahidjo, came from choiceless elections whose results were pre-ordained by their plebiscitary format. The mandates given Ahidjo's successor, Paul Biya, in 1984 and 1988 were in form much like Ahidjo's re-elections and gave Biya's regime the same results. This time, in 1992, there was opposition, offered mainly by John Fru Ndi, leader of the Social Democratic Party and spearhead of the movement to replace Paul Biya and endow Cameroon with democratic institutions. Official provisional results appeared to give the election to Biya, but international observers on the scene reported widespread vote fraud and irregularities of such magnitude that the national election commission delayed a formal announcement of the results until it could investigate the charges. On October 23 Biya was declared the winner and on November 10, was re-inaugurated as President. The opposition parties charged that the elections had been rigged and organized strikes and demonstrations in Douala, Bamenda, and throughout the Northwest Province. On October 27 the government placed the Northwest Province under a three-month state of emergency, and on the 29th, put Fru Ndi under house arrest. Whatever else the situation indicated, it was clear that the regime was not prepared to surrender power, or permit deviation from the pattern of leadership succession established in the early 1960s and continued during the presidencies of Ahidjo and Biya. What was that pattern, how was it created, and why does the regime cling to it with such tenacity?

Of the pattern, at least this much is certain: it took shape with the decision by the Ahidjo regime in 1962 to convert the country to a single party system, in the process forcibly integrating the opposition parties and imprisoning its leaders on various, transparently trumped-up conspiracy charges.[31] On September 1, 1966, with the dissolution of the main minority parties of West Cameroon, the newly renamed Union Camerounaise (UC) became the country's *parti unifié* (unified party), the *Union Nationale Camerounaise* (Cameroon National Union, CNU). It can be argued, as has Bayart, that this was all part of the emerging ruling class' "hegemonic project," that is, its attempt to give itself permanence by creating its own stable socio-economic and political base.[32]

The point of this Gramscian "project," of course, was to do anything - or virtually anything- necessary to preserve power in the hands of Ahidjo, his confederates, clients, and constituents - that is, the regime's nascent ruling class. This meant not only avoiding the uncertainties of electoral competition, but arranging periodic staged symbolic demonstrations of popular support ("elections," referendums, party holidays, public manifestations of thanks, etc.), and

---

[31] For details of this operation, see, inter alia, Willard Johnson, The Cameroon Federation (Princeton, NJ: Princeton University Press) 1970, pp. 243-256, 278-285.

[32] Jean-François Bayart, L'Etat au Cameroun (Paris: Presses de la Fondation Nationale des Sciences Politiques), 1979.

creating (among other things) an elaborate system of patronage that rewarded loyalty to the regime, and maintaining the political supremacy of Ahidjo's so-called "northern barons" while balancing the competing demands of various regional interests.[33] All this Ahidjo did with a mixture of political savvy, guile, and where necessary, brutality. Paul Biya, to whom Ahidjo handed power in 1982, certainly turned out to be no Ahidjo, but (to pursue the Gramscian argument) the hegemonic project begun by Ahidjo was so well along by 1984 that it benefited Biya- first by giving him a 99.98% vote in a January referendum on his presidency, and even more important, by providing him with critical regular Army support during the violent attempted coup of April 6-7, a coup that, ironically, probably had had Ahidjo's support. Biya, in his turn, took several pages from his mentor's book and perpetuated the Ahidjo pattern by being the sole candidate at the 1988 presidential elections, and by replacing Ahidjo's "northern barons" with his own (co-ethnic) group of "Beti barons" and a new North-South, East-West complex of clientilistic relationships. Seen in this context, the 1992 elections and its results came as no surprise: he was only protecting his class and its hegemonial project. Perhaps, had he been more politically astute, he might have (as did Senghor in Senegal) brought about a Gramscian "passive revolution," creating a narrow-spectrum multiparty system and the semblance of liberal democracy in which the ruling class could continue to hold the levers of power.[34] In

---

[33] Bayart, Ibid. pp. 185-235, passim.

[34] This is the thesis advanced by Robert Fatton, Jr., in his The Making of a Liberal Democracy: Senegal's Passive Revolution (Boulder, CO: Lynne Reinner, 1987)

the event, he did not, choosing instead, in the face of possible popular defeat, to announce his own results to the 1992 vote.

The Gramscian pattern, which was here extended to a possible full length because it is so intuitively attractive, does incorporate most of the salient elements in a persuasive description and analysis of Cameroon's succession schema. There is no need here to argue against the Gramscian pattern - I did not intend, in any case, to use it as a straw man - save to point out that its Achilles' heel is the premise of class. A credible case can be made, à la Pierre Ngayap[35], that however mutable its composition, Cameroon has a ruling elite, but that is a far cry from demonstrating empirically that it is also the core of a ruling class bent on its own "hegemonic project. At all events, the class premise cannot, without considerable distortion, encompass the role of Cameroon's very powerful ethno-cultural solidarities, at the very heart of Cameroon's recurrent oppositional crises. The Bamileke, the left ventricle of the old UPC resistance, remain uneasy and restive in the embrace of the regime, and it was Anglophone Cameroon and its long-standing grievances that originally animated the opposition from which John Fru Ndi and his party sprang. If there was a "hegemonic project," the regime and its problematic nascent class never successfully incorporated, or neutralized, some of the significant social forces which, during the early 1960s, stood hesitantly at the periphery of the Cameroonian polity: the Bamileke, the Anglophones, the radicalized intelligentsia, and the Christian communities of the south and center-south. And if Cameroon has a nascent ruling class, it stands to reason that it should have been able to muster, or mobilize, enough popular sentiment to give

---

35 Pierre Flambeau Ngayap, Cameroun, Qui gouverne? (Paris: L'Harmattan, 1983).

Biya, its evident champion, overwhelming support at its first, open, test of electoral strength. That Fru Ndi, himself an Anglophone, could (assuming for the sake of argument that the government's figures on the results are correct) garner enough votes for a close defeat, puts the solidarity, not to say the hegemonic project , of this "class" in serious doubt.

In this perspective, another, perhaps simpler pattern of succession can be argued. Put bluntly, my reading of the events, personalities, and actions of Cameroon's elite over the past thirty-odd years suggests that a) the Ahidjo regime, having held at bay and eventually defeating its pre-independence opposition, as well as wresting independence from the French, saw itself as the legitimate successor to the colonial state and thus, b) entitled to rule and to enjoy the fruits of its victories, something which naturally included tight control over the succession of personnel at the apex of local, regional, and national governmental structures. This also meant , of course, that Ahidjo would have the final say over his own succession, both according to the "rules" be created during his long term in office (which meant several re-elections by plebiscitary majorities) and in the end, by naming his own successor. In this respect, Cameroon was little different from the several other African states where founding fathers or their equivalents engineered their own succession: Senghor to Diouf in Senegal, Tubman to Tolbert in Liberia, Kenyatta to Moi in Kenya, Mba to Bongo in Gabon. At all events, having inherited a system that worked to preserve the ruling elite, it is hardly surprising that Biya should have followed the succession pattern laid down by his predecessor and mentor, even while creating his own regime (which, incidentally, eventually came to include a number of Ahidjo's former associates, not to say loyalists) with its own core of Biya fidèles.

I have argued elsewhere that at least until the attempted coup of 1984, Biya appeared willing to suit actions to his early rhetoric of liberalization and change the Ahidjo succession pattern.[36] That event may well have shocked him out of his reformist mode; thereafter, recognizing the brutal realities of the system he inherited, be simply adopted it lock, stock, and most of its barrel to keep himself and his people in power. (Certainly, the paranoid style of rule is not unknown in Africa.[37])

In sum, the Ahidjo-Biya succession pattern is less a "hegemonic project " than it is a pragmatic strategy to hold and maintain power not so much for a class, but for an elite whose membership has varied *en gros* with the single change of president, *en détail* positionally as the president and his closest associates change policy lines, seek to bring new talent into the fold, reward the faithful or punish the grossly incompetent or excessively greedy, try to balance debacle like the April 1984 coup attempt. Always, the aim is to preserve, and if possible, to enhance, the power of the regime and/or its head. Ahidjo succeeded quite well in this strategy during the almost twenty-three years he remained in power ; Biya, in his ten-year presidency , tried to emulate his predecessor (at least since 1984), but for reasons I need not rehearse here, nearly wrecked the whole system so carefully crafted by Ahidjo. He (Biya) managed to survive the 1983 destabilization plot allegedly hatched by two Army officers, Major Oumarou

---

36 "Leadership and Regime Changes in Perspective," pp. 20-52 In Michael G. Schatzberg and I. William Zartman, eds., The Political Economy of Cameroon (New York: Praeger, 1986).

37 See, inter alia, discussions of this phenomenon in Robert H. Jackson and Carl G. Rosberg, Personal Rule in Black Africa (Berkeley: University of California Press, 1982).

and Captain Salatou, fended off an apparent attempt by Ahidjo (during 1982-83) to re-acquire power, emerged alive (though somewhat traumatized) from the bloody April 1984 attempted coup, but then, even as he appeared to have solidly entrenched himself in power, proved incapable of dealing with rising demands for the democratization of the system. Unable, or unwilling, to placate or accommodate an opposition that nearly brought the country to its economic knees, he finally acquiesced in a presidential election that, as it turned out, he was unwilling to lose. In the process, Biya cast his regime even more deeply into the crisis which his maladroitness had helped bring about in the first place.

What led Biya into this current crisis? A brief look at its configurations may help explain both the nature of its threat to the regime and why Biya has been willing to resort to extraordinary means to deal with it.

It began with the transfer of presidential power from Ahidjo to Biya on November 4, 1982. Whether Ahidjo really meant to surrender all his powers to his hand-picked Prime Minister (as I argued at the time[38]), or simply intended Biya to be his marionette while he pulled the strings from the less exposed position of head of the national party, remains a matter of debate. What is clear is that Biya thought it real, and made promises in 1983 to liberalize the political system and restore confidence in the sagging economy - all to such effect that a "Cameroon spring" was definitely, though briefly, envisaged among the public at large. What is also clear is that the Ahidjo - Biya transition was also a succession crisis, one of much greater magnitude than Biya, or most his colleagues, had imagined. As subsequent events vividly demonstrated,

---

[38] "Cameroon: The Politics of Presidential Succession," Africa Report, Vol. 28 (1983), pp. 22-26.

neither Ahidjo nor many of his 'barons' were prepared to make way for a reformist leader, duly anointed though he may have been. At all events, the reforms were postponed when the old-guard's attempted *putsch* of April 1984 intervened, leaving hundreds of civilians dead and thousands wounded and bereaved. Again, without speculating further on Biya's state of mind after the attempted coup, his post-coup pronouncements underlined his realization that there were formidable dangers involved in reforming Cameroon, not the least of which came from what was left of Ahidjo's old guard loyalists. Thus, in February and March 1986, following nation-wide elections within the sole party, renamed the *Rassemblement démocratique du peuple camerounais* (RDPC), he replaced 70% of the party officials, including 54% of the regional chairpersons. His larger, promised reforms would now bring Cameroon into "the era of controlled democracy" by "slow, measured steps."[39]

The problem was that while Biya had, by 1986-87, weathered the succession crisis engendered by his accession to power in 1982, he had also raised expectations about political and economic reforms that his new program of "controlled democracy" could not hope to meet. To put it bluntly, the loyal opposition- those who had remained with him during the dark days of 1984 and were willing, thereafter to give him the benefit of their doubts - were fast becoming disillusioned. It did not help his cause that he backed and filled before finally accepting (in the eyes of many, on humiliating terms) an IMF/IBRD structural adjustment-cum-stabilization agreement; that he became "increasingly

---

[39] Jeune Afrique, 30 April 1986, cited in "Cameroon," p. 301 In Africa Contemporary Record 1986-87, Colin Legum & Marion Doro, eds. (New York: Africana, 1988).

isolated and indecisive, with much power entrusted to the unpopular clique that surrounds him"[40]; that, in what seemed a continuous, if vain, attempt to find stable combination of loyal helpers, he kept reshuffling his ministerial and advisory cards at a frantic pace[41]; and that all the government's austerity measures of 1987-88 were insufficient to balance the accounts, much less to restart the country's economic machine. In fact, Biya sank to such low public esteem that by the beginning of 1992 (as Milton Krieger reported[42]) "Conditions create an astonishing nostalgia for Ahidjo (partly sardonic, partly genuine) among some of the forces now aligned against Biya. A sense of ridicule for the 'small boy' in the shadow of the 'big man' attends Biya in favorite terms like 'Popaul' splashing the severely critical independent press which has emerged since 1990."

The current crisis itself, while partly rooted in earlier state-opposition confrontations and long-simmering Anglophone grievances, almost certainly dates from March 1990, when a Northwest Province bookstore proprietor, John Fru Ndi, sought to register his new party, the Social Democratic Front (SDF), with the Ministry of Territorial Administration under a 1967 statute which made that possible. Failing to receive a reply, he called for a march of support to be held in Bamenda on May 26. Tens of thousands of people responded, all was peaceful until later in the day, toward dark, when a skirmish between some of the

---

[40] Africa Confidential, Vol. 29, No. 4 (19 February 1988), p. 2.

[41] E.g., "Cameroun: Et maintenant?" Africa International No. 206 (June, 1988), p.p. 21-23.

[42] "Cameroon at Its Crossroads, 1992," Feb. 15, 1992, unpub. MS. I am grateful to Milton Krieger for letting me see unpublished versions of his fascinating eye-witness accounts of events in Cameroon during 1991.

marchers and elements of the uniformed forces at hand resulted in the deaths of six young people. The effects of the event outraced local outrage and stimulated the old loyal opposition to bring pressure to bear directly on the regime: Fru Ndi formally launched his SDF, then the National Assembly (in December) liberalized the process of party formation, so that by the end of 1991, almost fifty parties saw the legal light of day. The opposition's campaign also included instigation of months-long strikes and boycotts which since June 24, 1991 effectively closed down most of the country's urban centers for weeks at a time- what came to be called "*Operation Villes Mortes*" (Operation Dead Towns). Effectively stymied by the opposition, Biya (in December, 1991) finally convoked a small meeting of opposition party leaders, and on February 7, 1992, in what the government proclaimed as a generous concession to the popular will, formally announced parliamentary elections for March 1 next, to be followed by what he promised would be a free and open multiparty presidential election, these to be held in June, 1993. The latter date was later (under further pressure from the opposition) moved ahead to October 23 this year.

If the regime had hoped its concessions would be translated into a parliamentary mandate on March 1, it was both disappointed and embarrassed by its results: the government party (the CPDM) only obtained 88 of the 180 seats in an election marked by low turnout, especially in the North West Province constituencies when John Fru Ndi's SDF was known to be strong. The South West Province, Cameroon's other Anglophone area, registered an above-average turnout, but generally cast its vote for the opposition parties. More embarrassing still was the fact that 153 of the incumbent parliamentarians (including more than 60 belonging to the CPDM) were replaced, which, in effect, meant that the electorate - at best gloss- had only been willing to give the government's party 47% of the National Assembly's seats, or, counting only the votes cast, 43.1% of the total poll (1.83 million actually voted, only 58% of those registered). Seen in the rosiest possible light, the results hardly even added up to a lukewarm endorsement of the regime, its party, and president. In fact, it must have been evident to the President and his colleagues that their main line of defense against uncontrolled, involuntary succession, the Ahidjo-Biya pattern, was already crumbling at system's core.

What was left was the presidential elections, where some of the lost ground could be regained or, *in extremis*, the results more easily manipulated. The evidence strongly points to just such manipulation.

For our purposes, the current crisis can certainly be seen as a new succession crisis for Biya and his regime, threatening not only the survival of the Ahidjo-Biya political system, but also its succession pattern, a pattern that had successfully helped maintain power for the Ahidjo elite from 1958 to 1982, as it did for Biya and his regime, from 1982 to 1990. Whether the present regime will go the way of Africa's democratizing polities, or whether Cameroon will remain trapped in continuous political crisis - as is the case, for example, in Kenya, Togo, and Zaire - remains to be seen. However, if the democratic forces unleashed on the continent continue to gain ground, the next succession in Cameroon may well be a democratic one.

Chapter 6

Ahmadou Ahidjo in Retrospect, 2003

Following these 1984 and 1992 crisis profiles came Le Vine's assessment of Ahidjo's career as a touchstone for Cameroon, published as "Ahmadou Ahidjo Revisited" in Jean-Germain Gros' edited 2003 anthology *Cameroon: Politics and Society in Critical Perspectives.* Le Vine tracked Ahidjo as closely as any other scholar from abroad. He disclosed here (above and beyond a cocktail party meeting Nathalie recalls from 1960-1961) the two men's three formal interview or conversational encounters, in Yaounde 1959, Washington (D.C.) 1966 and Yaounde again 1971. The main text maps Ahidjo's life and career trajectory and provides a broad survey of politicians' and other scholars' views of Ahidjo beyond Le Vine's own. An appendix very usefully frames a chronology connecting his life with intersecting domestic and international events, continued past Ahidjo's death in 1989 to 1997 (when the text must have been written, then kept for this 2003 publication: how interesting it would, or will, be to read a similarly or even more detailed account of Paul Biya's presidential calendar). What emerges is a measured account of political leadership, largely free of references to the deeper anatomy of political power and structures, using significant Le Vine anecdotes back to 1959. His excursions into late 20th century scholarly debates find, rather than the emergence and reproduction of a monolithic "political class" around Ahidjo, the maintenance of "very powerful ethno-cultural solidarities" requiring constant management and realignment.

This "legacy" biographical sketch of Ahidjo, which duplicates some passages from Le Vine's 1992 paper reproduced above, balances praise and criticism from a variety of sources and compares Ahidjo and Biya, drawing on the 1992 text but adding another five years of experience and evaluation of Biya's presidency in light of Ahidjo's. The conclusion juggles circumspection and provisional judgment: "It is probably no compliment to the Biya regime to point out that in a great many ways, it was at first and still is much like the Ahidjo regime, in fact more so in the former's bad aspects than in its good ones." The current volume briefly revisits this topic in Chapter 7 and the Conclusion

Ahmadou Ahidjo Revisited

For the better part of the latter half of the twentieth century, Ahmadou Ahidjo dominated the political landscape of Cameroon, first from 1958 to 1960 as Prime Minister, then from 1960 to 1982 as President, and then for the next seven years until his death in 1989, first as his successor's nemesis and then (according to the regime), as a continuously malevolent presence in the political background. When Ahidjo finally died, (or so the story goes) Paul Biya breathed a sigh of relief, wished his predecessor's soul a speedy journey to hell, and immediately commissioned an appropriate eulogy to be read when the occasion presented itself. Nevertheless, with all that presence, in and out of office, Ahidjo remained something of an enigma to both outsider and Cameroonian insiders: no one ever quite knew what to make of him, or what he thought, or what he really wanted. This essay is unapologetically intended as yet another attempt to assess-and here reassess-Ahidjo and his legacy, although thirty years watching him from near and afar should provide me some cover for the effort. I have no ideological axes to grind, neither hated nor admired the man, and though for a time I was persona non grata in Cameroon (but unaware of it),[43]

[43] I only learned of this in 1971, when I returned to Cameroon to deliver a lecture at the University of Yaounde. Apparently, someone in the Presidency had got hold of a copy of the first French version of my first book on Cameroon (Le Cameroun du mandat à l'indépendance), took offence at something I had written about Ahidjo, and had me declared persona non grata for defaming the President. The Librairie Cle in Yaounde, which sold my book, was ordered to remove all copies from its shelves, which was done, and the books consigned to storage. My "p.n.g."

bore him no grudge and strove to be fair in my judgments about him.

Personality and Political Style

Ahmadou Ahidjo, President of Cameroon from May 5, 1960, until his resignation on November 6, 1982, died of a heart attack on November 30, 1989, in Dakar, Senegal. As of midyear 2001, notwithstanding the efforts of his family and some former friends in Cameroon, his remains had not been repatriated and reburied. (An Ahidjo chronology is appended to this essay.) Ahidjo was not an easy man to know. Publicly reserved, sparing of word and gesture, he admitted few people into his private world though he could be an agreeable companion and smoked, drank alcohol, and chewed kola in the company of his closest confidants. He shunned small talk, avoided social conversation if possible, and admitted that he disliked public debate and argumentation.[44] He rarely laughed

---

only lasted several months, and I was rehabilitated after cooler heads prevailed. My book was put back on sale, all of this happening without anyone informing me of it. I never found out just what it was that offended, or why I and my book were rehabilitated, or perhaps, forgiven?

[44] I met President Ahidjo three times, and on each occasion engaged him in extended conversation. The first time was in 1959, during my first visit to Cameroon, when I sought and obtained an interview with him in his office. The second time was during Ahidjo's state visit to the United States in 1966, when I sat next to him at a White House luncheon arranged by President Lyndon Baines Johnson. Johnson, who spoke no French (Ahidjo spoke no English), ignored his visitor for much of the lunch, preferring instead to talk with Sen. George Smathers (D., Florida); as a consequence, Ahidjo, who appeared glad to see me ("Aha! A friendly face!"), turned to me for conversation. The third time was in June 1971, a

in public, and though he was known to have used humor, irony, and sarcasm in some of his early speeches as a legislator in Cameroon, once he became President he maintained a grave and relatively humorless demeanor. Though a Muslim from the Muslim north, his Koranic education was shallow, and though he did undertake the Hajj in 1966 (and thus qualified for the title "Alhaji"), he avoided public displays of piety and had little to say on religious matters. At all events, whatever the other reasons he usually displayed this particular public face, there is little doubt but that he cultivated both his reserve and aloofness, since that gave him an air of imperturbability and impenetrability and undoubtedly heightened whatever fears people might have had in his presence. What it also did, of course, was to make him very difficult to read and to leave open the question, "Who was Ahmadou Ahidjo?"

The facts about his origins, upbringing, and education are sparse, and what we know about these matters is in some dispute. We are fairly sure that he was born in August 1924 (Victor Kamga says 1922; exact day unknown) of a Fulani Muslim mother, Astagabdo Ada Kano Garoua, who died in

---

visit arranged by Solomon Tandeng Muna, then Vice-President of the Federation. Ahidjo's admission about public debate and argument occurred during our third meeting. I should also add a somewhat embarrassed confession at this point: the research for this essay proved more difficult than I had anticipated. I have been writing about Cameroon for more than forty years, and I kept running into my own published work in many of the sources (both Cameroonian and non-Cameroonian) where I hoped I might find new insight into Ahidjo's rule and personality. If this essay, then, has a déjà-vu quality about it, I apologize, and can only claim that I tried as much as possible to avoid stumbling over my own footsteps.

Garoua on February 16, 1983. The identity of Ahidjo' s father is uncertain; he may have been one Youssoufou, and Ahidjo may have known him briefly inasmuch as Youssoufou is supposed to have died in 1929, when Ahidjo was five. Some who write about him claim Ahidjo was illegitimate, and argue that this fact in part accounts for his seeming social reticence; perhaps so, but since there isn't enough known about Ahidjo's paternity, suggestions about its effect are pure speculation. Abel Eyinga states (but without providing a name or corroboration) that Ahidjo's father was a Sierra Leonean, a former soldier in Britain's colonial army, who passed through Cameroon shortly after the end of the First World War.).[45]

At all events, the young Ahmadou apparently was reared by his mother and in 1939-aged fifteen-was finally admitted to the Ecole Primaire Supérieure (EPS) in Yaounde (Kamga claims he failed the entrance exams on his first try in 1937) from which he graduated in 1942 by the "little door."[46] That, in turn, led to a civil service position as radio operator (his official biographers later claimed "electrical engineer") for the

---

[45] Abel Eyinga, Introduction a La politique camerounaise (Paris: l'Harmattan, 1984), p. 161. Eyinga, whom I first met in Paris in 1959, was a steadfast opponent and vehement critic of Ahidjo, and has now become a critic of the Biya regime. '

[46] Victor Kamga, "Ahidjo et le mythe populaire," p. 17, in Kamga's Duel camerounais: democratic ou barbaric (Paris: l'Harmattan, 1985). Philippe Gaillard, Le Cameroun, Tome 2 (Paris: l'Harmattan, 1989), p. 11, explains that "the little door" (la petite porte) was a terminal departure out to work or whatever; "the big door, a narrow one, led to the Health School at Ayos, and thence, to the Medical school in Dakar." Gaillard adds that the paths to the Catholic seminary (in Yaounde) or to the Protestant teachers' school were not open to Muslims.

posts and telegraph (PTT) service and postings in Douala, Yaounde, and Garoua. One of Ahidjo's oldest foes, the author Mongo Beti (the nom de plume of Alexandre Biyidi), characterized Ahidjo as "illiterate" and ridiculed his lack of formal education beyond the EPS. The innocent stranger, argued Mongo Beti, could hardly imagine that every one of the President's silences, his studied hesitations, his lowered voice, his almost formulaic responses were due not to the wisdom of deliberation, but simply to his lack of education and the verbal poverty resulting from it. Embarrassed by his poor education, (according to Mongo Beti), he covered up; thus, his famous, much-admired reserve and dignity were little more than thin pretense.[47] This made him easily manipulable and thereafter, say Mongo Beti and Eyinga, all his important public statements and declarations were composed by others-first by the French, later by his smarter, better educated colleagues-and he only read the texts, usually badly. Ahidjo the puppet?

The accusation is hard to sustain, though it is true that initially, he was very much a creature of the French, especially the veteran Dr. Aujoulat who took him under his wing and helped get him up the political ladder (see below). But Ahidjo was not stupid, but cunning, and once in power, increasingly threw off the French traces. He was not well educated, and no master of the French language, and it is hardly surprising that he let others write his speeches for him-but so do most prominent politicians anyway. Mongo Beti overly ridicules Ahidjo for his lack of education, and it is difficult not to see a-measure of intellectual snobbery mixed in with Beti's dislike of the man. In my own conversations with Ahidjo I certainly

---

[47] Mongo Beti, Main basse sur le Cameroun (Rouen: Editions peuples noirs, 1984), p. 73.

found the reserve to be there, as well as obvious care in choosing words. But he was articulate, appeared to enjoy our conversation, and quite forthcoming in response to the questions I posed. And the intelligence was there, as well as mastery of detail and argument. On balance, I think Philippe Gaillard got it right:

> ... in a Fulani milieu where it paid to have connections to the nobility, a modest, even introverted postal employee had little weight besides the political leaders of the South, all better educated, older and already veterans of political or trade union activity, (as well as) brilliant orators. These scandal-mongers played a losing hand. They forgot that coming from an educationally impoverished region, of his age cohort, the little Fulani [Ahidjo] I was the most highly educated child of the North. And that the filter of the colonial school-to which the little or big feudal grandees, by refusing to send their own children and nephews, in effect sent Ahidjo—was an admirable instrument of selection.[48]

Jean-François Bayart, no admirer of either Ahidjo or his regime, may have come closest to characterizing his personality and style of ruling:

> In the unanimous opinion of those who have worked with him, M. Ahidjo fully assumes the responsibility of power and governs alone. He never seems to have an unofficial counselor, an eminence grise. Before making a decision, he multiplies his audiences and contacts, gathers the maximum differing points of view from his close

[48] Philippe-Gaillard, op. cit., p. 11. My translation.

advisors: (this is) a process which delays his choices and leaves him open to (charges of adopting) wait-and-see attitudes. This impression is accentuated by his preference for unspectacular results and the care he takes to avoid creating a stir. From which (arises) a certain preoccupation with managing his enemies and not crushing them when they are defeated-a (kind of) restraint that sometimes irritates his companions. As one of his partisans was supposed to have declared to the Head of State, "Better to be your enemy than your friend!" When he disgraces someone, he does so brutally, but such disgrace is generally of short term: M. Ahidjo uses men, casts them aside when they are no longer useful, and recalls them when they have been reformed (to his satisfaction). He is neither a nepotist nor a tribalist, and does not encumber the apparatus of state with his friendships. Difficult to influence, patient, cunning, secretive: M. Ahidjo's personality facilitated the regime's orientation to presidentialism.[49]

To which can be added the observation that when Ahidjo did make up his mind, he usually did forcefully, again, usually carefully preparing his ground beforehand and leaving little to chance. For example, when, in September 1966, he decreed the formation of the Union Nationale Camerounaise (UNC) as the country's sole legal party, he left the other parties' chiefs no choice but to join; they'd been warned (some of them already had been jailed earlier in 1962 for being politically recalcitrant), and thus immediately fell into line.

---

[49] Jean-François Bayart, L 'Etat au Cameroun (Paris: Presses de la Fondation Nationale des Sciences Politiques, 1979): 172-173. The translation is mine.

Equally, in 1972, when he decided that the federation had run its course, he left Anglophone leaders no choice but to endorse his referendum which, to no one's surprise, adopted the proposed unitary state by 99.97% of the votes.[50] The one major political decision that did not run true to form may well have been his last: to resign his office. I have elsewhere argued that he carefully prepared his departure,[51] and I still think so. However, I now think that he may also have thought a compliant Biya would allow him (Ahidjo), as titular head of the party, to pull strings from behind the scenes.

---

[50] Of the latter decision, Bayart noted:

> It is not necessary for the President to order the manipulation of the voting in any election. Administrative authorities, party officials, and the police make it their business to understand from his declarations the results needed and then to achieve them by whatever means necessary. The abrupt and arbitrary announcement by the Head of State on 2 May 1972 that within two weeks a referendum would be held on the question of abolishing a federal state ... meant, in effect, that within three weeks a Unitary State would be established with an overwhelming "Yes" vote.

Ch. 5, "The Structure of Political Power," in Richard Joseph, Gaullist Africa: Cameroon Under Ahmadou Ahidjo (Enugu, Nigeria: Fourth Dimension Press, 1978), pp. 80-81. The coming of the single-party system in Cameroon and the events of the 1966 transition are described, inter alia, in Bayart's L 'Etat au Cameroun, op. cit., pp. 109-140, in Willard Johnson's The Cameroon Federation (Princeton, NJ: Princeton University Press, 1970), pp. 243-256,278-285, and in my Cameroon Federal Republic (Ithaca: Cornell University Press, 1971), pp. 110-113.

[51] "Cameroon: The Politics of Presidential Succession," Africa Report 1983, 28: 22-26.

What Ahidjo had misjudged was Biya himself: the man he (Ahidjo) thought a foil and easily manipulable had ambitions of his own, with visions of a future in which Ahidjo played no part. Ahidjo apparently admitted as much in 1983.[52] At any rate, perhaps it was something Ahidjo could not have foreseen or understood; he had always played his subordinates with great skill, including an almost unfailing ability, year after year, to mix workable dosages—ethnic and regional balances--in his governing circle. Ahidjo, to all intents and purposes, had created Biya, and probably could not imagine that Biya the disciple would, or could, cross his master, nor probably, was it any consolation to Ahidjo that Biya had well and truly learned from his example.

Ahidjo could and often did act brutally, particularly against his political opponents and those who crossed him, and during his rule Cameroon's prisons housed a sizeable number of political detainees. Political murder has been put at his door, as has torture, and he has been accused of aiding and abetting a Cameroonian ethnocide. We will return to these matters later, when we consider the nature of "his" regime.

Why Ahidjo?

Philippe Gaillard was right: when Ahidjo entered Cameroonian politics it was dominated by the clever, better educated, even sometimes, "brilliant" men of the south. There was the redoubtable Louis-Paul Aujoulat, a French medical doctor deeply involved in Cameroon politics almost

---

[52] "Je me suis trompé. J'ai fait un mauvais choix. C'est un échec." (I made a mistake. I made a bad choice. It's a setback.) Quoted by Victor Kamga, op.cit. p. 24.

from the day he arrived in the colony in 1936 and Secretary of State for Overseas France in two French governments, the "Antillais" (West Indian) Jules Ninine, plus a phalanx of talented Cameroonians including Leopold Moume-Etia, Charles Assale, Daniel Kemajou, Charles Okala, Paul Soppo Priso, and above all, the extraordinary Prince Alexandre Ndoumbe Douala Manga Bell, German- and French educated, Chef supérieur (paramount chief) of the Douala, once a fervent opponent of colonialism and now, after World War II, become a member of the 1946 French Constituent Assembly and other local and metropolitan legislative and constitutive bodies. [53] How then did *le petit Peul* ("the little Fulani," a mocking title already used by his detractors in 1952), this taciturn, poorly educated northern "mediocrity" come to rise so high, so quickly, in Cameroon politics?

The characterization "mediocre" is Bayart's: he explains that Ahidjo became prime minister on February 18, 1958 because the French, who had engineered the rise and then the

---

[53] Richard Joseph offers a telling vignette of Prince Alexandre in Radical Nationalism in Cameroun (New York: Oxford University Press, 1977), pp. 79-84. Leopold Moume-Etia, one of the first trade union leaders of post-war Cameroun, has an unflattering portrait of the Prince in his Cameroun, les années ardentes (Paris: Jeune Afrique Livres, 1991), pp. 72-74. "If he'd had the will and the tenacity," wrote Moume-Etia, "really to give himself to politics and create a political party, he would have made Cameroun into a monarchy." I met Prince Alexandre in Douala in 1959 and found him frail, apparently literally drinking himself into the grave, but still gracious, generous, and articulate (in four of the seven languages he claimed to know). After our meeting, I could well understand why, at one time, he might well have been considered a likely candidate to become president of Cameroon; I could also understand why he had so many passionate supporters, as well as enemies.

fall of the hapless Andre-Marie Mbida, saw Ahidjo as a second-rank politician, someone who could easily be manipulated, blamed if things went badly and then replaced without second thoughts. (Richard Joseph even contends that High Commissioner Jean Ramadier was brought in [from Guinea] in early February 1958-as replacement for Pierre Messmer-specifically to remove Mbida and usher in Ahidjo.[54] Having done so, Ramadier was recalled three months later.) Besides, given the crisis which brought Mbida down, plus the ongoing UPC violence in the countryside (which, as Mbida's Minister of the Interior, Ahidjo had been left to manage), no one rushed to volunteer himself for Mbida' s job.[55] By that view, then, Ahidjo, already marked by his "apparent" mediocrity, was propelled upward by his French patrons, most likely as a temporary expedient, to be easily sacrificed later if the need arose.

---

[54] Richard Joseph, Radical Nationalism in Cameroun (New York: Oxford University Press, 1977), p. 343. Though Joseph offers no corroborative evidence for his proposition, it has found currency among Cameroon scholars. I have my doubts that it was all as stark as Joseph implies: I think it likely that Ramadier was sent because Messmer and Mbida proved unable to master the UPC rebellion and a more conciliatory line was seen necessary by Paris. Ahidjo, already in place as Vice-Premier and Minister of the Interior, was deemed ready to take on the job--or he may have so represented himself; Also, Joseph says that Ramadier came to Cameroun in 1957; not so: he was still in Guinea in early January 1958.

[55] Bayart, L 'Etat au Cameroun, op. cit., p. 49: "L'apparente médiocrité du personnage entra beaucoup dans sa fortune, et, si l'on peut dire, nul n'aurait donné très cher sa peau politique en ce mois de février." (The apparent mediocrity of the man had much to do with his fate, and, it can be said, during that month of February, his political skin was not worth much.) The translation was modified by the editor.

George Chaffard went Bayart one better: he argued that Mbida had been designated Prime Minister in 1956 precisely so that he would prove incapable of handling the job, and thereby advance Ahidjo's cause. Bayart, who appears to like conspiracy theories, did not buy this one. "It is possible," wrote Bayart, "that the colonial administration had noticed since 1956 the talents of the young deputy Ahidjo, but improbable that the long-term strategy of Paris would be based on so marginal a political figure."[56] Chaffard also mentions that at the time, there was also the so-called "Ahidjo option," by which Ahidjo (as temporary expedient) would have prepared the way for the later accession of Paul Soppo Priso. Soppo, says Bayart, at the time President of the Cameroon Assembly, figured in the (French?) calculus as the future leader of an independent Cameroon-as had Douala Manga Bell before him-but lost that footing when his attempts to reconcile the UPC and the French administration failed.[57] The "Ahidjo option" seems as improbable as the "Mbida option," if it can be called that, not because of Ahidjo's alleged "mediocrity," but because at the time it would have been much more politically economical to have moved Soppo directly from the Assembly to the Prime Ministry, thereby eliminating any unpredictable moves by Ahidjo.

Ahidjo's main critics-Chaffard, Bayart, Mongo Beti, and his opponents of the Left-all choose to explain Ahidjo's rise as due either to chance/force of circumstance or French manipulation, but not to Ahidjo himself though, to be fair, Bayart does acknowledge that the man had visible "talents"

---

[56] . Ibid., p. 47. The reference is to Georges Chaffard, Les carnets secrets de la décolonisation, vol. 1 (Paris: Calmann-Levy, 1967), p. 302.

[57] Bayart, note 46, in Joseph, Gaullist Africa, op. cit., pp. 46-47.

and some intelligence. In any case, in their view, whatever it was that propelled Ahidjo, it did not come from Ahidjo. Unfortunately, Ahidjo's official biographers and political hagiographers leaned all the way in the other direction, ascribing his rise to power, and his later "successful" Presidency, entirely to Ahidjo and to traits of intelligence and character that appeared entirely to have escaped the notice of his detractors. In the effulgent praise language appropriate to royal griots, he was described (for example) as "Father of the Nation, Pioneer of Negritude, Prophet of Pan-Africanism, Defender of African Dignity"[58] as well as the "[sic] quasi-charismatic ... personification of the national ideal ... [whose] boundless love for his country and noble sense of justice and the national interest predestined him ... for this exalting but difficult role of leading men."[59] This "pioneer of modem Africa," according to another authorized biographer, became an "enlightened guide for Africa." [60] (If "quasi-charismatic" sounds odd, it should, as it appears to be an awkward way by which Ahidjo's praise-singers dealt with the fact that Ahidjo was never genuinely popular, or inspired popular love, or really "connected" with his people. He was certainly feared and viewed with apprehension by friend and foe alike, respected by some, but was never, as far as I can recall,

---

[58] The quote is a translation from Mongo Beti's Main Basse sur Cameroun, cited in Joseph, Gaullist Africa, op. cit., p. 95. Beti does not exaggerate: I heard these terms myself in Cameroon.

[59] From the "Introduction" to *The Political Philosophy of Ahmadou Ahidjo* (Montel Monte Carlo: Political Bureau of the Cameroon National UnionlPaul Bory, 1968), pp. 11-12.

[60] From the dedication to Beat Baeschlin-Raspail, Ahmadou Ahidjo, pionnier de l'Afrique moderne (Monte Carlo/Yaounde: Paul Bory, 1968), unpaginated.

regarded with affection.) So if Ahidjo was neither the manipulable mediocrity, or illiterate puppet, or country bumpkin, of his detractors, nor the towering political genius and idealist portrayed by his griots, his rapid rise to the top of the Cameroonian political heap remains to be explained.

First of all, I think it must be conceded, as does Bayart back handedly, that Ahidjo in 1946 had political talent (albeit still raw and untested), plus considerable native intelligence, and that the combination must have made an impression on the experienced politicians of the Cameroon south. During our first conversation, in 1959, I asked Ahidjo about the early part of his career in politics, and he said he had been much impressed by the skill and self-assurance with which the politicians of the day conducted themselves. I should have asked him if this in fact inspired him to enter politics, but I did not, but if Bayart is right it was Pierre Rocaglia (together with Ahidjo, delegate to the new Cameroon Representative Assembly-ARCAM), who urged the young Ahidjo to take his first political steps in 1946, though his interest in politics already may have been aroused in 1945. (Abel Eyinga disagrees, quoting a Guy Georgy, the chief French colonial administrator in northern Cameroon from 1951 to 1955: Ahidjo had to be pushed into politics.[61])

---

[61] Abel Eyinga, "Historique de la francafrique en 5 dates" (suite), Le Messager, bftp://wagne.net/messager/0101/10histoire.httn, p. 3, sourced 3/23/01 :

> I held him (Ahidjo) in the highest esteem. I knew him since his beginnings .... He dreamed of becoming the chief of the postal service in the region, maybe even of the whole country, but above all, he didn't want to enter politics. But I kept pushing him into polities .... I got him elected to the Territorial Assembly. One almost had to

Small wonder that Ahidjo's interest was aroused (if that is what happened), since there was in fact a good deal about which to become excited, and the young Ahidjo, already marked because of his education, probably did not require much additional prompting: by the end of 1945 Cameroonians had already tasted the excitement of both wartime and post-war politics. During mid-1940, there was the tussle of divided loyalties (Vichy vs. Free France), won by De Gaulle's followers, and for a time—between August 1940 and recapture of Paris in 1944—Cameroon was at the very center of De Gaulle's Free France and Gaullist politics. On October 8, 1940 De Gaulle himself landed in Douala, and before long the colony became the launching pad for General Leclerc's brilliant military expedition across the Sahara into Libya and the Italian rear. In January 1944 De Gaulle convoked the Brazzaville Conference, and six month later, the French Communist-dominated trade union, the Confederation Générale du Travail (CGT) established a Cameroonian affiliate. In September 1944, strikes and violent demonstrations swept Douala, put down with force by the French administration.

So it is that in October 1947 Ahidjo is elected delegate to the ARCAM, and that same year, is defeated in a closed race for a seat in the Assembly of the French Union (created by the 1946 French Constitution), both candidacies benefiting from French endorsement and encouragement. He also begins to get acquainted with the big men of Cameroon politics: Aujoulat, Ninine, Mbida, Okala, Douala Manga Bell. In 1948, in Garoua (which he represents in ARCAM) he

---

get him votes by stuffing the ballot boxes! But it was for a good cause .... He was the natural son of a Fulani of modest origins ...

Jeune Afrique, no. 1410, 11 December 289. My translation.

delivers his first public speech. In Vol. 2 (p. 78) of the Cameroon Encyclopedia, there is picture of the young Ahidjo giving that speech; he looks to be no more than a teen-ager (though he was, in fact, 26 at the time), and visibly uncomfortable.[62] At any event, in April, he is credited with founding ASSABENOUE (Association Amicale de Benoue), a Garoua-based sociopolitical club for educated northerners. In 1953 he is designated a member of the Assembly of the French Union, and in 1954, he becomes a Secretary to the Assembly, inscribed as a member of the [independants d'Outre-Mer along with Senghor and L.-P. Aujoulat. In May 1955 he is Vice-President of the Territorial Assembly (ex-ARCAM), and in December 1956, heading another of his creations, the Union for the Growth of North-Cameroon (UENCUnion Nord-Cameroun) he contests Jules Ninine's

[62] Encyclopedie de la Republique Unie du Cameroun. Four Volumes, boxed (Douala: Nouvelles Editions Africaines, 1981). I hope I didn't misread Ahidjo's look: Arouna Njoya, one of Ahidjo's oldest friends and advisors, once told me that at least until 1951, Ahidjo was always very nervous when speaking publicly. The caption does say that it was Ahidjo's first public speech, and Arouna had a pretty good memory. [Note: The Encyclopedia became available in a limited edition to subscribers in the national party, the legislature, the higher ranks of the administration, and the community of foreigners. Needless to say, failure to subscribe could be interpreted as mark of disloyalty and/or lack of friendship toward the regime. I own set no. #678, which includes a bronze medallion with Ahidjo's likeness on the cover of Vol. I. Since the subscription cost about US $200, I was willing to risk being thought both disloyal and unfriendly and obtained my set through informal channels for US $40.00. A note in Vol. I says thal 10,300 sets were printed. If all the sets had been subscribed, the take would have been over $2.0 million. I was told at the time that the edition had been "oversubscribed."]

seat to the French National Assembly and is soundly beaten. Back in the Cameroon Legislature (the ATCAM, reconstituted as a Legislative Assembly later) in January 1957, he is elected President of the Assembly by acclamation. And, in the first Cameroon government under the Loi Cadre in May 1957, he is named Minister of the Interior in Mbida's cabinet, and then, nine months later in February 1958, prime minister. From ATCAM backbencher in 1947 to prime minister in 1958: a vault from bottom to top in ten years is a pretty impressive political ascent in anybody's book. But did he do it on his own or was he pushed (catapulted?) or pulled up?

As usual, the answer lies somewhere between the extremes. At various points Ahidjo certainly had help, and guidance, and good counsel, and most important, the intercession of people who counted and could further his career. The French were there, though at the beginning it was the local Frenchmen and southern-based "evolué" Cameroonians involved in the territory's politics, like Aujoulat and Rocaglia and the "Antillais" Jules Ninine and Mbida who perhaps saw in him the core of a manageable future northern Cameroonian leadership. But there was also ambition, and an eye for opportunity, and native intelligence. Sometimes he overreached himself, as he did when he challenged Jules Ninine for the latter's French National Assembly seat in the north; I think it a measure of "the little Fulani's" resilience that the experience of defeat only derailed him briefly, going on as he did within a month to become the local assembly's president.

Finally, his stepping into Mbida's prime ministerial shoes in 1958 was neither the result of an "Ahidjo option" nor an "Mbida option," as I suggested earlier. What did happen was that at the beginning of 1958, Ahidjo was so positioned that he was able to take advantage of the opportunity presented by Mbida's inability to deal with the UPC uprising, the consequent impatience of France's Minister of Overseas France, Gerard Jaquet, and. the actions of Jaquet's replacement for (Cameroon High Commissioner) Pierre Messmer, Jean Ramadier. I think that, of all those who have searched this history for ways of detracting or adding to Ahidjo's repute, Robert Mortimer, who sought neither, got it more right than anyone.

Mortimer recounts how the UPC's terror campaign mounted in intensity during 1957, and after Mbida gave a fiery speech in Reuben Um Nyobe's home village of Boumnyebel denouncing the UPC as a "clique of liars and demagogues" and threatening further repressive measures, the rebellion spread to the Bamileke region where, on the night of December 13-14, a Bamileke member of the territory's Legislative Assembly, Samuel Wanko, was murdered along with six others. Mbida flew to Paris to seek military reinforcements, but met resistance from both French politicians and Cameroonian leaders who still hoped for reconciliation with the UPC. However, not even the Bishop of Douala, Thomas Mongo, who had managed to see Urn Nyobe in person, could persuade him to accept a cease-fire. According to Mortimer:

> Jaquet, Minister of France d'Outre-Mer, took a personal dislike to Mbida and began to think his government was the principal obstacle to peace. But Mbida was backed up by the High Commissioner, Messmer, who, like Roland Pre before him had been converted by the course of events from leniency to a tardy and heavy-handed repression. Like Buron in 1954 and Deferre in 1956, Jaquet decided that a new High

Commissioner would stand a better chance. At the end of 1957 he promoted Messmer to be High Commissioner for AEF, and replaced him in Cameroon with Jean Ramadier, who had just come back from Guinea. He instructed Ramadier to sound out the political possibilities and then report back. Ramadier exceeded these instructions spectacularly. Virtually his first action on arrival in Yaounde was to persuade Ahidjo's Union Camerounaise to desert Mbida's government. Left without a majority, Mbida resigned, and on 18 February Ahidjo was elected prime minister in his place. Mbida flew again to Paris, and filled the lobbies of the Palais Bourbon with his complaints.[63]

If Mortimer has it right, and I think he does, the key to Ahidjo's accession to power was first and foremost Ramadier who, had he obeyed Jaquet, would have left Mbiya in place. Mortimer interviewed Jaquet, and the phrase about Ramadier exceeding his instructions clearly came from Jaquet, not Mortimer. Even given Jaquet's dislike of Mbida and

---

[63] Robert Mortimer, France and the Africans, 1944-1960, a Political History (London: Faber and Faber, 1969), p. 300. Bayart's account of these events ("L' Accession au pouvoir de M. Ahidjo") is on pp, 23-52 in his L 'Etat au Cameroun, op. cit; Richard Joseph's version is on pp. 342-350 in his Radical Nationalism in Cameroun, op. cit.; and in my book, The Cameroons from Mandate to Independence (Berkeley: University of California Press, 1964), pp. 162-171. Ramadier was recalled three months after he'd been sent not because he had accomplished the task of putting Ahidjo in place, as even Mortimer hints, but because he'd exceeded his instructions and because he became insubordinate thereafter. What saved him from disgrace were his Socialist credentials, which included being the son of the distinguished Socialist Paul Ramadier.

conceding that he might well have wished Mbida out of office, Jaquet would not have acted until Ramadier had reported back to him as instructed. Moreover, there was Ahidjo, Mbida's Vice-PM in charge of the Interior, to take the fall if needed, and if the mediocrity thesis holds, then he could have been easily sacrificed. But Ramadier either thought he had been charged with bringing Mbida down,[64] or took it upon himself to do what he thought Jaquet would have wanted, or he simply did what he thought necessary under the circumstances. I think the second and third interpretations equally credible, and in any case, absent additional evidence there is no warrant for interpreting Jaquet's dislike of Mbida as an order to remove Mbida and substitute Ahidjo for him. A 1964 letter from Ramadier to Abel Eyinga, cited by Eyinga and later, by Victor Julius Ngoh, reinforces my impression but does not resolve the issue. However, it does confirm that Ahidjo did not like Ramadier or his appointment, that he (Ramadier) thought he had approval to remove Mbida, and that he saw an Ahidjo government as a transitional operation (transitional to what?) designed to pursue negotiations with Um Nyobe:

> At the end of 1957 everybody understood that Mbida hung on only because of us [the French government] and that all solutions to the Cameroonian problem had to start with his elimination [from office] .... I must admit that, before my departure [for Cameroon], I'd considered looking into the possibility of having Mbida depart without delay, and that that was approved. The choice of

[64] Jean Ramadier's biographers, Jacques Larrue and Jean-Marie Payen, argue the former alternative. See their book, Jean Ramadier: Gouverneur de la décolonisation (Paris: Karthala, 2000).

> Ahidjo had been, in a way, imposed on me. I met him in Paris; our first contact was rather brutal. Ahidjo did not conceal the fact that he opposed my appointment solely because I was a socialist, and I made it clear to him that there were socialists and socialists. But to be more precise, the solution that I envisaged, absent an immediate detente with Um [Nyobe], was to put in place a transitional Ahidjo-Assale tandem ... a transitional government whose only role would be to enter into negotiations with Um and the internal opposition.[65]

And so Ahidjo moved stage front and center in Cameroon on February 18, 1958, and there he stayed for the next 24 years, impelled (both before and after that year) in part by those who helped set him on his way, in part by his own talents and intelligence, and in part by opportunities presented by the circumstances in which he found himself. Ahidjo, as it turned out, was in the right place at the right time, and despite their mutual dislike of one another, took the opportunity offered by the new High Commissioner. As for Ramadier's "transition," he was not around long enough to oversee either a transition to another government (perhaps

---

[65] In 1964 Eyinga and Ramadier corresponded, and the letter in question was dated 15 October 1964. It is reproduced in full in Abel Eyinga's Mandat d'arrê pour cause d'élections (Paris: Harmattan, 1978), pp. 104-105. The translation is mine. A poor and hence misleading translation (e.g. "entente" instead of detente of parts) of the letter appears in Victor Julius Ngoh, Cameroon 1884--1955: A Hundred Years of History (Yaounde: Navi group, 1987), p. 154. It has been suggested to me that the letter is a fraud, authored by Eyinga, not Ramadier. I think not; having met Eyinga and thought him an honest person, I give him the benefit of the doubt.

even one led by Soppo Priso, which is what he may have had in mind in the first place) or, as it turned out, Cameroon's transition to independence.

A third conundrum that needs revisiting, along with my own revisit of Ahidjo's political style and rise to power, is the nature of the regime that bore his name, and it is to that I now turn.

The Ahidjo Regime

It is probably no compliment to the Biya regime to point out that in a great many ways, it was at first and still is much like the Ahidjo regime, in fact more so in the former's bad aspects than in its good ones. [66] I admit the judgment is mine, but happily, here I am seconded by Philippe Gaillard, Victor Kamga, Mark Delancey, and most recently, by Joseph Takougang and Milton Krieger? [67] The UPC, which had always denounced the Ahidjo regime as a neo-colonial creation with Ahidjo in the role of fanioche (puppet) of France and French interests, predictably saw Biya's as no less compromised and ultimately, just as malign.[68] The reflexive

---

[66] Part of this section is derived from my paper on "Crisis and Democratic Succession in Cameroon," presented to the panel on "Succession in Africa" at the annual meeting of the African Studies Association held in Seattle, Washington, November 20-23, 1992.

[67] Gaillard, op. cit.; Kamga, op. cit., Mark W. Delancey, Cameroon: Dependence and Independence (Boulder, CO: Westview/Dartmouth, 1989), p. 70; Joseph Takougang and Milton Krieger, African State and Society in the 1990s: Cameroon's Political Crossroads (Boulder, CO: Westview, 1998), pp. 62-85, passim.

[68] See, for example, the special issue of Peuples noirs, peuples africains (Nos. 55, 56, 57, and 58, together; Jan.-Aug, 1987) on "Le

judgment of the UPC aside, this much is certain: that after the abortive coup of 1984, the Biya regime shelved its early moves at political reform and a more relaxed overall political atmosphere, adopting many of the most authoritarian methods of Ahidjo's rule including heavy-handed police operations, physical assault on opponents, imprisonment without trial, extra judicial punishments including torture and death. However, to say that Biya used pieces of the Ahidjo template in constructing his own regime does not reveal much about Ahidjo's construct except to remind us of its repressive ways. So what kind of a regime was it, in fact? Was it a Gramscian "hegemonic project," as Bayart claims? Was it a "ruling elite," or ruling class, per Pierre Ngayap? Was its example so persuasive that Biya could find one no better or more useful? Or was it, above all, a wholly murderous, evil, and perhaps even genocidal regime, as (most recently) François-Xavier Verschave strongly suggests?

The last charge needs to be addressed first because, if true, it should color all subsequent judgments and analysis about the regime, and because, being of recent vintage, it has gained currency and wide dissemination. And it is not a new charge, since the UPC and its friends have described the Ahidjo regime in such terms since 1958. At all events, put briefly, Verschave, in reviewing the 1958-1963 French-Cameroonian campaign against the UPC rebellion in the

---

Cameroun de Paul Biya: autopsie d'un chaos annoncé." Mongo Beti was editor of this journal. Among other items, the issue contains an odd piece intimating that an Israeli neutron bomb was responsible for the 1986 deaths of over 1,200 farmers living on or near the shores of Lake Nyos, in west Cameroon, all of whom had in fact died from a poisonous gas emitted by the lake. See also the Cahiers Upécistes, Jan.-March 1985, no. 21, and the article on the 1984 attempted coup d'état (pp. 6-120).

country's Bamileke area, approvingly quotes a French helicopter pilot, Max Bardet, to the effect that they (the combined French-Cameroonian forces) "massacred between 300,000 and 400,000 persons. A true genocide. They practically annihilated the race. (It was) spears against automatic weapons. The Bamileke didn't have a chance .... Their villages were razed, a bit like Attila."[69]

Verschave offers no corroboration for these figures, but accepts them implicitly as he argues (in a chapter entitled "Massacres en pays Bamileke"-massacres in Bamileke-land) the common complicity and guilt of the new Ahidjo regime, the French government and its colonial military, all organized and directed from Paris by Verschave's bête noire, Jacques Foccart. Foccart, who apparently met Ahidjo when both served in the Assembly of the French Union, also becomes, in Verschave's account, one of Ahidjo's chief puppeteers. There's little question about the ferocity with which both the rebellion and the military campaign to suppress it were waged, and that in the process, thousands were killed, wounded, or rendered homeless. Verschave calls it a rehearsal for Vietnam, and I can offer eye-witness testimony to the

---

[69] Max Bardet and Nina Thellier, OX Cargo! (Paris: Grasset, 1988), quoted without page reference by François-Xavier Verschave, La francafrique: Le plus long scandale de la République (Paris: Stock, 1998), p. 91. My translation. The latter book gained additional currency because of the international publicity given a suit-by three incumbent African Presidents-against Verschave and his publisher for alleged defamatory statements made in his latest book, Noire silence (Paris: les arènes, 2000). In May 2001 the French court before which the case was being heard threw out the suit, deciding that the old 1871 law on which it was based, was now itself in contravention of the Statutes of the European Union.

brutality of both sides.[70] However, I'm convinced the counter-insurgency campaign never attained the Vietnam-like intensity or scope claimed by Verschave, nor (as my own research indicated) did the casualty count exceed 1,000 military and somewhere between 10,000 to 20,000 civilian casualties sustained between 1955 and 1962. In fact, Verschave even undermines his own argument in a cryptic footnote:

> The number cited by Max Bardet remains hypothetical inasmuch as the survivors, with the support of Cameroonian and foreign historians, are themselves reluctant to evoke the horror [of the massacres]. This cast of mind, which has lasted a third of a century, by itself testifies to the scope of the massacre.[71]

---

[70] I was in Cameroon in October 1959, and visited a Bamileke village that had just been "liberated" by the UPC's Armée de libération nationale kamerunaise (ALNK). The villagers had been accused of collaboration with the authorities, and for that sin, over 150 men, women, and children had been hacked to pieces. Two days later, I was shown the fresh corpses of several dozen alleged "terrorists" shot by the French-Cameroonian forces: a number of women were included, as were several children barely over ten years old. For whatever it's worth, I traveled around in the Bamileke and Cameroon highland areas of western Cameroon during the years 1960 and 1961 and found few traces of the rebellion, much less people who described it in Verschave's terms. The rebellion had pretty much died down by 1961, being reduced to sporadic outbreaks, what with Urn Nyobe's death and the splits within the UPC itself in which several of its leaders had changed sides and "rallied" to the Government in 1960 and 1961.

[71] Verschave, op. cit., p. 91 (footnote #2). My translation. My own figures are drawn from my chapter "Cameroon (1955-1962)" in D. M.

Suffice it to point out that this is classic illogic: the claim that the absence of evidence about something is the best proof of its existence. Further, Verschave need not have gone to such lengths to make the case for an Ahidjo-Foccart collaboration, and in his zeal to assign guilt for the horrors of the rebellion and exculpate the U.P.C., he went overboard. And, in any case, admittedly bloody as was the rebellion and its suppression, the facts about the counterinsurgency campaign do not also warrant a charge of genocide, or wholesale massacre, against the Ahidjo regime. It was brutal, but not genocidal. (I also wonder who those "Cameroonian and foreign historians" are/were who helped "the survivors" repress their memories.)

As I suggested earlier, it was clear that after 1984, and including the events before and after the 1992 presidential elections, the Biya regime was not prepared to surrender power even by constitutional means, or permit deviation from the pattern of rule established by the Ahidjo regime in the early 1960s.

Of that pattern, at least this much is certain: it took shape with the decision by the Ahidjo government in 1962 to convert the country to a single party system, in the process forcibly integrating the opposition parties and imprisoning its leaders on various, transparently trumped up conspiracy charges. On September 1, 1966, with the dissolution of the main parties of West Cameroon, the newly renamed Union Camerounaise (UC) became the country's parti unifié (unified party), the Union Nationale Camerounaise. Bayart has argued that this was all part of the emerging ruling class' "hegemonic

---

Condit, Bert H. Cooper, Jr., et. al., Challenge and Response in Internal Conflict, Vol. III (Washington D.C.: American University, Center for Research in Social Systems, April 1968),pp. 239-267.

project," that is, the attempt to give itself permanence by creating its own stable economic and political base.[72]

The point of this Gramscian "project," of course, was to do anything – or virtually anything – to preserve power in the hands of Ahidjo, his confederates, clients, and constituents, that is, the regime's nascent ruling class. This meant not only avoiding the uncertainties of electoral competition, but arranging periodic staged symbolic demonstrations of popular support ("elections," referenda, party holidays, public manifestations of thanks, etc.) and creating (among other things) an elaborate system of patronage that rewarded loyalty to the regime, and maintaining the political supremacy of Ahidjo's so-called "northern barons" while balancing the competing demands of various competing regional interests.[73] All this Ahidjo did with a mixture of political savvy, guile, and where necessary, brutality.

Biya certainly turned out to be no Ahidjo, but (to pursue the Gramscian argument) the hegemonic project begun by Ahidjo was so well along by 1984 that it benefited Biya-first by giving him a 99.98% vote in a January referendum on his Presidency and, even more important, by providing him with critical regular Army support during the violent attempted coup of April 6-7, one that, ironically enough, appeared to have Ahidjo's support. Biya, in turn, took several pages from his mentor's book and perpetuated Ahidjo's pattern by being the sole candidate for the 1988 presidential elections, and by replacing Ahidjo's "northern barons" with his own (co-ethnic) group of "Beti barons" and a new North-South, East-West network of clientelistic relationships. Seen in this context, the flawed 1992 and 1997 elections came as no

---

[72] Bayart, L' Etat au Cameroun, op. cit.

[73] Bayart, ibid., pp. 185-235, passim.

surprise: Biya was only protecting his class and its hegemonic project. Perhaps, had Biya been more politically astute, he might have—as did Senghor in Senegal-brought about a Gramscian "passive revolution," creating a narrow-spectrum multiparty system and the semblance of liberal democracy in which the ruling class could continue to hold the levers of power with popular approval.[74] (I do not know if Ahidjo thought of the possibility in 1982 when he was about to turn power over to Biya, but I doubt it.)

Bayart's Gramscian analysis is intuitively attractive because it does incorporate most of the salient elements in a persuasive description and analysis of the Ahidjo regime's pattern of rule. There is no need here to argue against the Gramscian pattern-I had not intended, in any case, to use it as a straw man-save to point out that its Achilles heel is the premise of class. A credible case can be made, à la Pierre Ngayap, that however mutable its composition, Cameroon has a ruling elite, but that is a far cry from demonstrating empirically that this elite is the core of a ruling class bent on its own "hegemonic project." My point is, that premise cannot, without considerable distortion, encompass the role of Cameroon's very powerful ethno-cultural solidarities, themselves at the very heart of the country's recurrent oppositional crises. The Bamilekes, the left ventricle of the heart of the old UPC resistance, remain uneasy and restive in the embrace of the regime, and it was Anglophone Cameroon and its long-standing grievances that originally animated the opposition from which John Fru Ndi and his party sprang. In recent years, many dissatisfied Bamilekes have made common

[74] This is the thesis advanced by Robert Fatton, Jr., in The Making of a Liberal Democracy: Senegal's Passive Revolution (Boulder, CO: Lynne Rienner, 1987).

cause with the Anglophones' political projects.[75] Consequently, if there was a "hegemonic project," as Bayart contends, the regime and its problematic nascent ruling class never successfully incorporated, or neutralized, some of the significant forces which, during the 1960s, stood hesitantly at the periphery of the Cameroonian polity: the Bamilekes, the Anglophones, the radicalized intelligentsia, and the Christian communities of the south and center-south. (Not even having a Catholic and former seminarian as President has done the trick for Biya, as witness the angry exchanges between Cardinal Tumi and Biya's regime. And if Cameroon has a nascent ruling class, it stands to reason that it should have been able to muster, or mobilize, enough electoral strength to give Biya, its evident champion, overwhelming support at its first open test of electoral strength in 1992.) Moreover, the class solidarity, much less its hegemonic project, was seriously compromised by the Ahidjo-Biya succession crisis. The logic of Bayart's argument would have predicted a seamless, peaceful transition, since it was simply a matter of one part of the same team passing the baton to another. Not so, of course: the succession not only witnessed mutual charges of "betrayal" by the principals of one another, but also re-exposed the system's older north-south, Anglophone-Francophone, Muslim-Christian rifts, fault lines that Ahidjo had more or less kept covered up.

---

[75] For details of the Anglophones' dissatisfaction and the Fru Ndi phenomenon, see Takoungang and Krieger, op. cit. I offer anecdotal support for the stories of the Bamilekes' political troubles: a dozen of over thirty Cameroonian asylum cases (brought before the US immigration courts) in which I've been involved as an expert consultant or witness have had to do with Bamileke who fled political prosecution in which their identity as Bamileke played a role.

In this perspective, another, perhaps simpler pattern of regime rule can be argued. Put bluntly, my reading of the events, personalities, and actions of Cameroon's political elite over the past forty years suggests that (a) the Ahidjo regime, having held at bay, and eventually defeating, its pre-independence UPC opposition, as well as wresting independence from the French, saw itself as the legitimate successor to the colonial state and thus, (b) entitled to rule and enjoy the fruits of its victories, something which naturally included tight control over all the levers of power in the system-personnel, the structures and institutions of rule-making, coercion, persuasion, and symbolic output-at all levels from the village to Yaounde. It had, after all, the example of the Fifth Republic, inaugurated in 1958 and crafted as something new for France, a Presidential system with a subordinate, not sovereign, legislature. By that example and the logic of the independence transition, which took place under the auspices of the Fifth Republic, the single "unified" party made sense, as did the personalization of power and a muscular presidentialism. So too did minimum tolerance of opposition, and (in a perversion of the French system) the creation of a structure of official repression, complete with its own secret police (SEDOC and its successors), eminence grise (Jean Fochive), prisons for political criminals, and non-judicial punishments (for details, see special and annual reports of Amnesty International; Human Rights Watch, and the US Department of State).[76] It

---

[76] The essays in the book edited by Richard Joseph, Gaullist Africa: Cameroon under Ahmadou Ahidjo (Enugu: Fourth Dimension Publishing, 1978) all accept the premise that Cameroon under Ahidjo was a part of France's "indirect colonialism," replicating the worst aspects of

made sense for Ahidjo and his regime, and it appears to have made equal sense to Biya arid his.

In sum, the Ahidjo-Biya regime pattern is less a "hegemonic project" than it has been a political strategy to hold and maintain power not so much for a class, but for an elite whose membership has varied en gros (wholesale) with the single change of president, en detail (retail) positionally as the president and his closest associates change policy lines, seek to bring new talent into the fold, reward the faithful, punish the "disloyal" or grossly incompetent or excessively greedy, or clean house after a crisis or debacle like the April 1984 coup attempt. Always, the aim is to preserve, and if possible, to enhance the power of the regime and/or its head. Ahidjo succeeded quite well in this strategy during the almost twenty years he remained in power. Biya, now in power for almost as long, has tried to emulate his predecessor (at least since 1984), but for reasons I do not rehearse here nearly wrecked the whole system so carefully crafted by Ahidjo—and may still do so if he keeps increasing opposition to him and his policies.

Conclusions

My revisit of Ahidjo has been, of necessity, narrowly focused and unfortunately, limited in scope. What has hampered the revisit is that it had been difficult to get an objective view of the man and his works, given the ideological lenses through which most of those who have written about him have done so. There are still all too few published, authoritative works on the Ahidjo era, and those

---

the De Gaulle regime including its neo-colonial designs. Joseph's essay on "The Gaullist legacy," pp. 12-27, is to the point.

of us who are interested in it, keep finding (and citing) each other's work in our own. In this revisit, I sought to emphasize points which I think are frequently overlooked or neglected: that the Ahidjo "enigma" was not so much the product of his shortcomings than of his calculations; that Ahidjo was much more his own man than he is usually credited with being; that his rise to power was not French-propelled, but in considerable part his own, as well as the product of circumstance; and that the Ahidjo regime was not so much an "hegemonic project" than an ongoing effort by Ahidjo (and his successor) to keep political power and its attendant prerogatives for themselves and their clients, kinsmen, and supporters. These are not, admittedly, earth-shaking revelations, but I offer them to help clear analytical space for the other essays in this volume.

An Ahidjo Chronology

Date	Ahidjo	Cameroon	French/ International Context
1924, August?	Born in Garoua of Astagabdo Ada Kano Garoua, father unknown (?)	Cameroon is League of Nations Mandate	
1925, ?	Death of Yousouffou, putative father. Enters koranic school in Garoua directed by Mal Oumarou		
1932, ?	Enters regional (elementary) school in Garoua		
1937, February	Fails CEPE, entrance exam for Yaoundé Ecole Primaire Supérieure (E.P.S.)	Mandessi Bell founds *Union Camerounaise*	
1938, February	Passes CEPE and entrance exam for Yaoundé E.P.S.	Paul Soppo Priso founds *Jeucafra*, 1st legal Cameroon political org.	
1940, October 8	Studies at E.P.S.	De Gaulle debarks at Douala; Free French rule	France under German occupation, Vichy rule
1942, ?	Graduates from Yaoundé E.P.S., probation period at Douala		
1943	Posted to Yaoundé Beroua, Mokolo		
1944, January	Posted to Garoua		Brazzaville Conference
1945, July	Becomes interested in politics (?)	Trade union protests UN Trusteeship for Cam.	W.W. II ends
1946	Enters politics	Houphouet et al. create RDA	Nov., League of Nations ends; Cold War begins

Date	Ahidjo	Cameroon	French/ International Context
Jan. 1947 (–1952)	Delegate to Cam. Rep. Ass'y (ARCAM) from Benoue district		
1948, April	Founds ASSABENOUE (Assoc. Amicale de Benoue)	UPC founded by Um Nyobe, et al.	
Mar. 1952, Dec. 1956	Re-elected to Cam. Terr. Ass'y (ATCAM); VP ATCAM,1955–'57		
1953	Designated Councillor to Assembly of French Union		
1954	Sec'y to Ass'y of Fr. Union; becomes member of I.O.M. group		
1955, May	V.P., ATCAM	UPC rebellion begins	
1956, December	Creates UENC (Union pour l'Evolution du Nord-Cameroun); beaten by J. Ninine for seat in Fr. Nat'l Ass'y		June: Loi Cadre grants partial self-gov't to 'colonies
1957 May 9	(Jan.) Elected Pres. ALCAM; Vice-PM, Min. of Interior in Mbida gov't	"Etat sous tutelle;" (Feb.) J.Ramadier arrives; First Cameroon gov't (Mbida)	
1958, February May September 13	Resigns from Mbida govt; Invested as PM by ALCAM *Union Camerounaise* founded	(Feb.) Mbida resigns; Ramadier replaced by X. Tore Um Nyobe killed	French constitutional crisis: DeGaulle & 5th Republic arrives
1959, March July	 Meets Foncha in Buea		UN votes independence for Cameroon
1960, Jan. 1 May 5	 Sworn in as 1st Pres. of Cam	Cam. becomes independent (Feb.) Const. adopted	

Date	Ahidjo	Cameroon	French/ International Context
1961, Feb. 11 October 1 October 1 November 11	 Granted *pleins pouvoirs* Pres. of Cam. Federal Rep. Press conf. on "great national unified party"	(Feb.) UN plebiscite in Brit. Cam.: So. Cam votes to join Cam. Rep., N. Cam. votes to join Nigeria. (Oct.) Reunification: Cam. Federal Republic	
1962	Moves toward single party system	June: Main opposition leaders reject "national unified party," are jailed. E. Ouandie returns to lead UPC guerrilla struggle	
1965	Re-elected President Reconciles w/ Archbishop Zoa, received by Pope in Rome		
1966	Heads "unified" party, *Union Nationale Camerounaise*	Single-party state inaugurated	Ahidjo state visit to US
1970, March	Re-elected President; moves toward "reinforced" presidential regime	July: E. Ouandie arrested; Aug: Bishop Ndongmo arrested—"Holy Cross Plot"; in prison until '75	Georges Pompidou, president of France (1969)
1971, Jan. 13		Ouandie, 3 others executed; UPC rebellion dissipates	

Date	Ahidjo	Cameroon	French/ International Context
1972, May 20 June 2 July 24	Supports ending federation Decrees division of Cam. into 7 provinces	(May) Referendum on ending federal state (June) Const. of United Cam Rep. promulgated	
1975, June	Names Paul Biya 1st PM of United Cameroon Republic		Valry Giscard d'Estaing, Pres. of France (1974)
1979, June	Reconfirms Biya as PM, names him constitutional successor		
1982, Nov. 2 Nov. 6 December 11	Resigns as Pres.of Rep., but elected VP of UNC Central Com. Retires to Nice-Grasse (France) Returns from Nice; meets w/ Pol. Bureau of UNC	(Nov. 6) Biya takes oath as President	François Mitterand, Pres. of France (1981)
1983 Jan. 23–30 February 16 March 3 May 14 June 18 July 19 August 23 November 1	Tour of provinces Death of Ahidjo's mother Awarded Dag Hammarskjold peace prize Radio address angers Biya Meets w/ northern ministers, asks them to resign; maybe plot to retake power? Leaves by ordinary AF flight Resigns as President of UNC Named as co-conspirator in plot v. Biya (along w. Salatou & Ibrahim)	(Jan.) Biya announces mottoes of his admin.: rigor and morality; tours provinces, Feb.–June '83. (June 20) Biya meets w/ French Pres. Mitterand, gets blessing (Aug. 8, 18) arrests of Capt. Salatou & Cmdt. Ibrahim; Biya claims plot vs. him & state	

Date	Ahidjo	Cameroon	French/ International Context
1984, Feb. 23–Apr. 5 Apr. 6–8 April 14	Trial of plotters, incl. Ahidjo (Apr. 6) Broadcast from Monte Carlo blaming Cameroonians. Abidjo charged as instigator ofattempted coup, issues denial, asks to be left in peace	(Jan. 14) Biya elected President of Republic (Apr. 6–8) Attempted military coup vs. Biya. (Apr. 27–May 10) trial of accused coup-makers.	
1984–89	Exile (Nice, Spain, Senegal)	1988, Biya elected Pres.	Mitterrand re-elected (1988)
1989, Nov. 20	Death in Dakar, Senegal		
1991	Presidential decree rehabilitating political opponents who died in exile, including Ahidjo		
1992		Biya re-elected President in tarnished & disputed election	
1997	Gov't comission agrees to return property confisctaed from Ahidjo in 1984; Ahidjo's son, Mohamadou, signed to receive it. Remains remain in Senegal.	Biya re-elected President in elections bycotted by opposition	Jacques Chirac, Pres. of France (1995)

Chapter 7

Cameroon in *Politics in Francophone Africa*, 2004

The three previous writings were more "occasional" than central later in Le Vine's career. His time in Cameroon diminished after the 1981-1982 Fulbright semester, with only lecture appearances in 1983 and 1989, his last time there, as part of wider African tours for the United States Information Agency between his regular teaching semesters. The itinerary thereafter reveals a comparative political scientist's work at a high level of scholarship and also practice. Emory University's Carter Center appointed Le Vine to the international observer team for Ghana's 1992 presidential election. He was a consultant to Eritrea's constitutional commission, 1995-1996. Subsequent travel before and after his formal academic retirement in 2003 added the Czech Republic, Cyprus and Northern Ireland to his African circuit for international crisis management assignments. The United Nations, the Center for International Understanding and the International Peace Academy were among his sponsoring agencies.

These cumulative experiences yielded Le Vine's career-defining book published just past his seventy-fifth birthday, *Politics in Francophone Africa* (2004). Cameroon study was the original cornerstone and Le Vine's own and others' scholarship originating there figured prominently as points of departure and reference for writing he distributed quite evenly between Cameroon and the other thirteen nations covered. The scope of its 400+ pages vastly outstrips any possibility or intent for summary coverage here, but two important Cameroon features stand out: Le Vine's last published (and as far as I know unpublished) commentaries on both Cameroon's polity at large and the Ahidjo and Biya presidencies, summarized but not reproduced here, and an excursion into what he termed "parapolitics" in a brief passage striking enough in its Cameroon application to be reprinted in this chapter.

On the first point, he had written more than once about the 1982-1984 turmoil and Biya's subsequent debt to his 1984 military saviors. But he had noted at that time that Cameroon was just the fifth African country where the transfer of power from a founding president to a successor was literally "constitutional" (if not peaceful), and now in 2004 ranked it among Africa's civilian "administrative-hegemonic" regimes. This category was Naomi Chazan's from the standard politics text she edited, *Politics and Society in Contemporary Africa* (1988); the two were close colleagues and friends, collaborating first (as noted above) in the University of Ghana's political science department around 1970, again at length when Le Vine was a visiting professor at Chazan's Hebrew University in 1978, and multiple other times in Israel, the U.S.A. and elsewhere. This designated for Le Vine (2004, p. 203) a polity with "more or less pragmatic rulers…willing to find ways of including key interest group (ethnic, regional, class, occupational) leaders in the decision-making process, as well as giving their judiciaries and bureaucracies, including the technical apparatuses, both room within which to function and some autonomy vis-à-vis each other." And directly to the question of Ahidjo's and Biya's performances in the presidency (2004, p. 217), "Biya did, all in all, manage to keep Ahidjo's administrative-hegemonic regime intact, though never at the levels of effectiveness it reached under Ahidjo… Biya never proved as guileful…nor able to find the effective, pragmatic balances between accommodation and coercion, reward and punishment that had been Ahidjo's hallmark." Although he failed to note that his own 1992 speculation (see Chapter 5 above) about a possible democratic succession had not come to pass, Le Vine's enduring skepticism about Biya registered in the way the paragraph he opened by acknowledging Biya as Ahidjo's constitutionally legitimate heir (cited just above) closed with these words: "whether the regime will survive in its present form is another question."

The second theme with important Cameroon bearings from *Politics in Francophone Africa* emerged in Chapter 10, "In the Shadow of the State: The Domain of Informal Politics" and in the specific domain he called "parapolitical." Le Vine's early Cameroon writings had emphasized conventional description and analysis of statecraft, in legal-constitutional, political and bureaucratic channels, with the intricacies of interest group and patron-client networks factored in, and these were carried forward in his comparative studies. But his widening lens over the decades and his political science discipline's greater attention to the varieties and anomalies of political experience beyond the control of state actors surfaced decisively in the 2004 text, a scholarly direction Chazan informs me they had explored together since they were colleagues in Ghana a quarter century before. Thus (2004, pp. 305-306), this "third domain…intersects both high and deep politics (the latter more than the former)…[and] is characterized by its inhabitants' purposive distantiation, even often relative autonomy, from the state and its formal institutions and agents…All of this is in large part, though not exclusively, the politics of civil society, the politics with which most people have daily contact and that, in most countries, encompasses the greatest volume of political transactions."

This passage and its further elaboration, not just in the 2004 book but in a "Current Project" he described in his 2006 *curriculum vitae* as a "Book on 'Parapolitics: The Theory and Practice of Non-Formal Politics'" he didn't live to write, aligned Le Vine's late contributions to enquiry identified with the distinguished younger Cameroonian scholars Achille Mbembe and Célestin Monga and to non-Cameroonian Africanists like Bayart (originally a Cameroon specialist), Stephen Ellis, Béatrice Hibou and Janet Roitman. The vocabulary of parapolitics "thickened" the sense of the state's operations and impacts on those it governed, in the broadest social science context of Clifford Geertz's "thick" description, and likewise covered defiance of and resistance to the state, in the sense conveyed by James C. Scott. In ways he had not done before, Le Vine used Bayart, Mbembe, Monga et. al. as 2004 sources immediately following his introduction to parapolitics quoted just above, and cited the anthropologists (but not African specialists) Geertz and Scott in the book's bibliography.

There's a pronounced trajectory in all this. Le Vine, a prominent early-career pioneer of state-centric political science for Cameroon and Africa, moved in mid-career through thematic and locale-specific varieties of comparative study in his field, and then responded with sensitive antennae as scholarship's elders and cadets prompted more multidisciplinary channels for his own established repertoire. In contrast to the writings principally attuned to the operation of Cameroon's and then many of Africa's other states ("high politics") in early writings, the less visible, always negotiated and often contested character of parapolitics, and the fluid, complex nature of the citizen-subject nexus, registered more strongly in Le Vine's fully mature scholarship.

The best way to demonstrate this late strain in his work for Cameroon is now to reprint material from *Politics in Francophone Africa*, pp. 310-313, directly below. Le Vine's visit to the West Province village of Bana in 1980 turned into the thickest account of parapolitics the 2004 book provides. It describes the dense connections between Cameroon's annual "Cultural and Development Association" village celebrations and the more metropolitan habitats and even foreign terrains such villages cultivate. The quarter century's interval between Le Vine's 1980 experience at Bana and its 2004 recounting produced a couple of minor textual errors, but his anecdotal flourishes personalize and dramatize the basic story and indeed reinforce its parapolitical character by suggesting the village's shrewd purpose in having him, a senior and well-connected foreign scholar, fetched from Yaounde to Bana in a "chauffeur-driven Mercedes." It is an informative and engaging read.

Celebrating Bana: A Personal Narrative

If the data are to be trusted, the Bamiléké and their ethnic cognates make up around 30 percent of Cameroon's population. Their home country–designated as *le pays Bamiléké* (or *le pays dites-Bamiléké* –"the so-called Bamiléké country") by French and British ethnographers and generally accepted as such by the Bamiléké themselves-is a large, densely populated, hilly area located in Cameroon's southwest. Its inhabitants are mainly concentrated in the Southwest and Northwest Provinces, with significant numbers in the neighboring Littoral Province as well. The area contains about one and one-half million of the roughly four million Bamiléké in Cameroon, clustered in and around four main towns (Bafang, Bangangté, Bafoussam, and Nkongsamba, the Northwest Province's capital) and in some ninety named chiefdoms of various sizes and importance, each with a main town to which the chiefdom gives its name and where the chief has his official residence or palace. The Bamiléké have made their mark on Cameroon by the vigor and commercial acuity of their people, the avidity with which their sons (and more recently, daughters) have taken to both modern education and politics, the press of their demographic expansion, the lingering effects of sporadic and sometimes deadly conflict with their Bamoun neighbors, and the fact that the radical nationalist rebellion that shook the country from 1955 to 1962 played out the second part of its guerrilla stage in the Bamiléké homeland. During the 1990s and early years of the twenty-first century many Bamiléké were again on the defensive as the Biya regime came to see some of their leaders and notables – with some justification – as part of its opposition.

By size and population Bana town is small to medium-sized; when I visited in 1980, it probably had no more than about ten thousand in residence. But, as I soon learned, it had importance far beyond what its size and population would indicate: it was a small commercial and political powerhouse that was able, as it turned out, to put on an extraordinary three-day extravaganza (on February 3, 6, and 7, 1980) commemorating, as Bamiléké tradition dictated, both the death and the funeral of its late king (technically, *fon*) Hapi II, and the enthronement of his successor, King Hapi III.

I was told that the royal family – by name Hapi or Happi, spelled either way – had invited some five thousand people to the second part of the event, the enthronement on February 7, including the sultan of Bamoun; a clutch of neighboring chiefs; high government officials; members of the diplomatic corps from Yaoundé; and important notables, friends (like myself), allies, and businesspeople from all over the country. From my vantage point it appeared as if almost all the invitees had come, plus, by right, a huge number of the Bana themselves from both near and far. (I had been invited because I was friends with one of the Hapi and a visiting Fulbright professor at the University of Yaoundé, To my considerable pleasure, the Hapi even sent a chauffeur-driven Mercedes to fetch me from Yaoundé.)

We witnessed the royal installation, the elaborate "traditional" *hommages* (honors) paid the new king, dancers in costume from all over the Bamiléké area, and various age-grade and traditional Bamiléké societies parading and dancing in their finery. We heard musical ensembles (both traditional and modem) and the sultan's trumpeters and his personal praise-singer in full throat, and we saw displays of royal art, masks, cloth, and costumes that were brought out only for the most important ceremonial occasions. An elaborate lunch (huge mounds of chicken, lamb, goat, yams, rice, vegetables, fruit) was set for three thousand of the guests on that third day, and we sipped orange squash (soda), beer, and chilled French Moët et Chandon champagne convoyed up from Douala a week earlier (I was told the wine needed a week to settle down after the bottles' bumpy, hundred-mile truck ride from the coast).

It was, in all, both stunning and memorable, representing a deliberate exhibition of wealth, power, and good fortune far beyond what one would expect of a chiefdom that normally presented a modest front to the world. Long after it was over, 1 asked my hosts and several well-informed Bamiléké friends to explain the discrepancy and the reasons for what seemed to me to be an ostentatious, even extravagant display. First of all, 1 learned that it was not the royal Bana treasury that paid for the event, but Bana businesspeople and households throughout the country, many of whom vied with one another to see who could raise the largest sums. Second, my hosts explained to me in gentle rebuke that what was done was neither extravagant nor ostentatious, but befitting of the occasion, the guests, and the need to impress the visitors.

The event was an opportunity to remind the visitors that Bana was more than it seemed, that it could mobilize its hidden wealth to invite – read "command the presence of" – the great and powerful of the land. The presence of the sultan of Barnoun, a traditional grandee of national importance with whom the Bana had forged an informal alliance, emphasized the point. The message was that here was real influence, and that it could be translated into benefits for the Bana – and its friends – at the seats of local and national power. No one should forget, my interlocutors emphasized, that the Bana already had three of the Hapi in Yaoundé, individually and collectively representing Bana interests and ensuring that it would be heard by the government: Louis Kemayou Hapi, former mayor of Nkongsamba and ex-president of the eastern and national legislative assemblies; Jean-Claude Hapi, a son of the late King Hapi II and counselor at the presidency and the ministry of foreign affairs; and Daniel Kemayou Hapi, vice president of the court of appeals in Yaoundé.

Finally, and perhaps most important, the event was a way of renewing the ethnocommunal solidarities on which Bana stood and to reassert publicly what the ethnic home meant to both those "at home" and those "abroad." Pride, and even some arrogance, was certainly involved, as well as the renewal of trust and reinforcement of the subtler structures of ethnic kinship. It did not surprise me that not only the older Bana, but also other Bamiléké whom I encountered in Cameroon frequently spoke of retiring "at home": *au village, chez moi.*

My visit to Bana was in 1980, over twenty years ago, and I have no way of knowing if the Bana still have the measure of influence of which they reminded their guests, or even if they had as much political influence then as they claimed. What is important is that Bana, while unusual in its role as a mini powerhouse of wealth and influence, was not alone among Bamiléké communities in its willingness to display its ethnic pride in the accumulation of wealth or to use the multiple structures and channels of the parapolitical domain to protect and enhance its position.

The Bana chiefdom, one of ninety similar Bamiléké units, is technically part of the substructures and institutions of Cameroonian local government, all of which fall under the jurisdiction of the national ministry of territorial administration and ultimately are subject to the power of the presidency of the country. Part of that power is exercised through the *fon* himself; according to Decree No.77/245, made law in 1977, all "traditional chiefs" became auxiliaries of the administration. This was something of a trap for the chiefs because those who were seen to use the power of the office too much to advance that of the state could attract the opprobrium of their people, "who have more and more difficulty in separating the fon's incontestable power from the secular, party-political and therefore moral contestable power of the state."

Although this summarily describes the formal linkages between periphery and center, it does not, and obviously cannot, encompass the multiple parapolitical ties between the Bana and those in the corridors of power; nor can it encapsulate the loose and resilient but effective network of solidarities and reciprocal obligations on which the Bana – and the Bamiléké at large – can call when needed. Needless to say, these non-formal ties and networks are as real and consequential as those described by the formal structures of politics – perhaps even more so. Clearly Bamiléké – "Bami" – is more than an ethnic identity: it represents salient membership in a socially and politically important group whose interests, demands, concerns, and national presence, manifested in both the formal and informs political domains, have to be taken seriously by any Cameroonian regime whatever its provenance.

Chapter 8

The Bakassi Dispute, 2007

His unpublished archival materials yield the final Le Vine excerpt selected for this volume. It has very little connection to our earlier texts. But it covers a Cameroon issue that was incipient when he first arrived there, became periodically explosive, lingers today, and will have a bearing into the future.

This is a 18 July 2007 background paper, written after his retirement, about the "Bakassi Dispute" in the coastal border area where energy resources so strategically and competitively engage Cameroon and Nigeria. A 2002 International Court of Justice ruling had favored Cameroon in this decades-long dispute, but conflicting claims and tensions remained along a porous border stretching north to Lake Chad and south off-shore. Le Vine's audience is not specified, although the (originally) inked words "Various Colleagues" appended to the "Questions Posed by" language in the first H section's typescript heading argues strongly for a panel or forum with multiple attendees (the inclusion of a second "H" section and other anomalies indicate the text's informal rather than academic purpose, for which he would have edited more carefully; this version retains the original text), and a few interpolations indicate Le Vine's post-delivery additions to the text. Given the text's informality, perhaps the Carter Center or some equivalent agency was hosting Le Vine as a featured consultant, among scholars, industry people whose interests were practical, and Cameroonians from (to the degree this distinction makes sense) the private and public sectors. Regarding the "practitioners" interests: anyone who's spent time in Douala's international airport in recent decades knows how many petroleum geologists, technicians, managers and entrepreneurs have traveled to Cameroon or through there to its Gulf of Guinea and inland neighbors, working in strategically important ways this Bakassi material illuminates.

Whatever the text's venue for delivery and its circumstances, its discussion of petroleum and energy politics at large provides a good reading of Cameroon as an "African crossroads." Its scope and details also confirm Le Vine's stature among the country's authoritative sources, from its inception to its most current affairs. He drew on archives and newspapers for the presentation and appended a comprehensive bibliography for the principals to consult. He included the historical micro-politics of the relevant area's ethnic groups and factored in the contemporary resistance movements to national governments in Nigeria's oil delta and among Cameroon's anglophone secessionists. He covered the place of treaties involving earlier European and now African sovereign states, the United Nations and the International Court of Justice in the diplomatic, legal and political arenas. He placed commercial-industrial and human rights interests alongside governmental concerns in the dispute. The document lacked an environmental assessment, but was otherwise comprehensive, framing lessons and recommendations for all parties to consider.

The result was a multidimensional briefing on Cameroon's current strategic niche in its region, and on the continental and global implications for the country's leaders of any future actions and decisions. Dating from Le Vine's late seventies, likely his last writing directed specifically to Cameroon, it was cumulatively seasoned in many of his scholarly arenas, and addressed the country's condition in the larger context called for in 2007 as comprehensively as his earliest writings did during its formative years nearly half a century earlier. It fittingly capped his Cameroon career, and completes this collection of his writings.

A. Description

1. Physical/geographic

The Bakassi peninsula is a ca. 665 km^2 (194 sq. mi.) projection into the Gulf of Guinea consisting of a number of low-lying, largely mangrove covered coastal islands located roughly between latitudes 4°25' and 5°10'N and longitudes 8°20' and 9°08'E. Bakassi lies ca. 60 km east by northeast of Mount Cameroon, and ca. 50 km south by southwest of the key Nigerian port of Calabar, the largest western coastal town in Nigeria (Bakassi commands strategic access to Calabar, which is not only being developed as Nigeria's Export-Processing Zone and Eastern Command Headquarters of the Nigerian Navy, but also has rich hydrocarbon and fish resources.). While Cameroon has discussed building some roads into Bakassi with the Mixed Cameroon-Nigeria Commission set up as a result of the 2002 ICJ decision; it does not yet appear to have done so, although the oil/gas companies operating the area may have started such construction. Anyway, surface access is by sea or across the several adjoining rivers (See attached maps of Bakassi and Cameroon coastal areas).

2. Human settlement

Historically, Bakassi has been inhabited by Nigerian Efik/Ibibio peoples, though currently, the peninsula's population includes Cameroonian coastal peoples. Total population is in dispute, estimates ranging between 150,000 and 300,000, the numbers growing during the Nigerian/Biafran (civil) war (1967-70), diminishing during the Nigeria-Cameroon hostilities over the peninsula during the mid-1990s, and according to some reports, increasing once more as hydrocarbon exploration started up again in the area in late 2002. Almost all Bakassi inhabitants live by fishing, and the fluctuating availability of fish in the coastal and riverain areas has also impacted the size of local populations.

[***Political Question:*** Has Cameroon taken steps to see that Bakassi inhabitants will benefit from oil/gas finds in the area so as to avoid the local violence/disturbances in the Niger Delta arising from alleged maldistribution of profits from the Delta oil extractions? ***VLV Says:*** It appears that some vague promises to this end have been made by the Cameroonian government, but one is entitled to be skeptical, given the government's record of failure to live up to its promises to the World Bank about the uses of profits from the Cameroon-Chad pipeline to benefit populations impacted by the project. Ref: Amnesty Int'l 2005 report, *Contracting out of human rights: The Chad-Cameroon pipeline project.*]

3. Geological/resources: oil & gas

The peninsula itself is commonly described as "oil-rich," though in fact no commercially viable deposits of oil have yet been discovered on it. However, the area has aroused considerable interest from oil companies in light of the discoveries of high-grade crude oil reserves elsewhere along the Delta and southern coastal areas both onshore and offshore in the territorial waters of Nigeria. At least eight international oil companies, plus Cameroon's national oil company, the Société Nationale de Hydrocarbures (SNH) are involved in exploration concessions in the area, both onshore and offshore, and recent discoveries of viable deposits in both the Douala and Rio del Rey (geologic) basins have spurred further exploration.

There are <u>no reliable estimates of the possible oil or gas reserves</u> in the exploration concessions, but while potential discoveries may not match those in Nigeria, optimistic projections suggest that enough oil may be found to reverse the downward trend in Cameroon oil exports, at the low level of 60,000 barrels a day (bbl/d) in 2005, down from a high of 84,800 bbl/d in 2000. (Cameroon is sub-Saharan Africa's sixth largest oil producer, with reserves estimated at 400 million barrels.)

(For exploration and possible areas of deposits, ***See*** the petroleum-economist. com map of Equatorial Guinea exploration concession areas, and Total's "Cameroun Domaine Minier" map, attached.)

The following companies are involved in hydrocarbon exploration - resumed in late 2002 after a hiatus of some ten years - in the Bakassi peninsula, the Bakassi-area, and the adjacent offshore areas (mainly in the Rio de Rey and Douala Kribi-Camp Basins):

SNH (Cameroon)

TotalFinaELF/Pecten (France, multinational)

Conoco/Phillips (US)

Shell (Société Shell du Cameroun, multinational, affiliate of Royal Dutch Shell)

Perenco (US, with multinational partners)

Grynberg Petroleum Co. (US, multinational)

Tullow Oil (UK)

Addax Petroleum Cameroon, Ltd. (Canada, multinational)

Fusion Oil (Australia)

(The Cameroon government has partially privatized the SNH in conformity with World Bank dictates, but continues to use the SNH to supervise and license oil/gas exploration and exploitation.)

B. History of the Dispute

1. An Efik "kingdom" (chieftaincy) was founded in Bakassi ca. 1450, and subsequently incorporated within the framework of the "kingdom" (paramount chieftaincy) of Old Calabar.

2. During the "scramble" for Africa, representatives of Queen Victoria signed a Treaty of Protection with the King and Chiefs of Old Calabar on September 10, 1884. This enabled the British to exercise control over the entire territory of Old Calabar, including Bakassi. In 1960, when Nigeria became independent, Bakassi (according to the Nigerian claims) became *de facto* a part of Nigeria. The location and extent of the Cameroon-Nigeria boundary (including possession of Bakassi) had never been permanently settled, and thus became an increasingly contentious issue between the two countries. (See Timeline for specifics of the boundary issue.)

3. Two subsequent developments brought the issue to the surface: First, the issue arose during the 1967-70 Nigerian civil war when close to 5,000 Biafran refugees made their way into Bakassi to escape the fighting. Some refugee leaders apparently thought they were in Cameroon, part of the over 20,000 Efik/Ibo refugees that sought, and were granted, temporary asylum in Cameroon. Second was the rich oil and gas discoveries in the Nigerian Delta and adjacent coastal areas during the early 1970s, leading to the first Cameroonian license contracts for oil and gas exploration/ concession/production offshore Bakassi and Douala (Kole Marine, 1976; Ekundu Marine, 1977; Boa Bakassi, 1979).

4. Claims and counter-claims by Cameroon and Nigeria over possession of Bakassi led to increased tension between the two countries, which in turn brought them to the brink of war in 1981, provoking armed clashes both during the 1977-81 and early 1990 periods. To emphasize its claim and to fight Cameroonian "incursions" into the area, Nigeria brought some 3,000 - 4,000 (exact numbers are unavailable) troops and naval units into Bakassi and the adjacent region; Cameroon brought equal numbers of forces to their side of the border, ready to fight the Nigerians if need be. There were several clashes between the units on both sides, beginning with that involving an armed confrontation in which 6 Nigerian soldiers on patrol were killed in 1977 when Cameroon's SONARA refinery, near the border, was opened. After repeated failures to resolve conflict peacefully, the Nigerians eventually sought a military solution, and in December 1993 occupied some parts of the Bakassi; in reaction, Cameroonians attacked the occupation forces, resulting in several deaths and large-scale destruction of property. In February 1996, the Nigerian occupation forces again clashed with Cameroonian troops. Unverified reports claimed additional clashes and casualties on both sides totaling anywhere from ten to 200 killed/wounded, including a Cameroonian claim that Cameroonian naval forces had sunk three Nigerian ships.

5. In response, Cameroon brought the matter before the International Court of Justice on March 29, 1994. Since both the onshore (including Bakassi) and offshore marine boundaries were at issue, the international oil/gas companies temporarily suspended exploration pending the decision of the Court.

6. The ICJ delivered its verdict (for details see below, #D) on October 10, 2002, by which it awarded Bakassi to Cameroon.

7. Despite the efforts of various Nigerian, Bakassi, and Anglophone Cameroonian civil society groups to invalidate the ICJ's decision, including an abortive attempt to declare a secessionist "Democratic Republic of Bakassi," on June 13, 2006, Presidents Biya (Cameroon) and Obasanjo (Nigeria) finally resolved the issue in talks led by UN Secretary-General Annan in New York. The Nigerians agreed to abide by the Court's judgment and to withdraw their troops from Bakassi and its environs. On August 14, 2006, a ceremony marked the formal handover of the northern part of the territory to Cameroon, the remainder to stay under Nigerian civil authority for two more years, during which the rest of the Nigerian troops and officials would withdraw.

C. Politics, pre - ICJ Decision

1. Clearly, absent the discovery of substantial real and potential oil/gas deposits on both sides of the Nigeria-Cameroon boundary, Bakassi would not have become an issue for both governments. The record shows sporadic clashes between Cameroonian and Nigerian fishermen over fishing rights in and around Bakassi during the 1960-2002 period, but these appear to have been treated as inconsequential by both sides and more or less easily resolved.

2. On the Nigerian side, willingness to resolve the territorial issue, beginning with the Gowon-Ahidjo entente in 1975 (the Maroua Declaration), fluctuated with the several

changes in military (and civilian) regimes after the 1967-70 Nigerian civil war as new regimes installed by military coups used the Bakassi issue to display their toughness, or alternately, their goodwill toward neighboring Cameroon and the international community. For Gen. Murtala Mohammed, who overthrew Gowon five weeks after the Maroua Declaration (and rejected it), as for the Babangida and Abacha regimes, toughness and protection of Nigerian oil rights and territory were important policy stances; finally, it took the Obasanjo presidency to agree to plead its case before the ICJ, and to endorse the Court's decision. Moreover, the armed clashes in/around Bakassi between 1993 and 1996 proved inconclusive for both sides, and the military option lost its luster, at least for the Nigerians.

3. The Cameroon governments, first that of Ahmadou Ahidjo until 1982, and its successor Biya regime to the present, never wavered in their claim on Bakassi, deploying diplomatic and legal means, plus the threat (and apparent use) of military confrontation, to back its arguments . Resort to the ICJ also indicated that the Cameroonians understood that despite the inconclusive results of the military confrontations of 1993-1996, their military could not hold on indefinitely in the face of superior Nigerian forces, and that their best chance of resolving the issue, absent a workable diplomatic agreement with the Nigerians, lay with the Court. In 1962 Cameroon went to the Court to challenge one result of the 1961 UN plebiscite in British Cameroons - the Northern Cameroonians' decision to join Nigeria - and lost; this time they had a much better case and a much better chance of winning.

D. The ICJ's Decision

1. While Cameroon's approach to the Court was motivated mainly by the Bakassi dispute, the Court also dealt with other points of friction along the Cameroon-Nigerian border, including its northern reaches near Lake Chad, the maritime boundary into the Gulf of Guinea from Bakassi, and agreed to include Equatorial Guinea's submission about its maritime boundary. My summary focuses on the Bakassi aspects of the decision.

2. The case was extremely complex, requiring the Court to review diplomatic exchanges dating back over 100 years. Nigeria relied principally on Anglo-German correspondence dating from 1885, as well as treaties between the colonial powers and indigenous rulers of the area, particularly the 1884 Treaty of Protection.

3. Cameroon pointed to the Anglo-German treaty of 1913, which defines spheres of control in the region, as well as two agreements signed during the 1970s (specifically, the Yaoundé II Declaration of April 4, 1971 and the Maroua Declaration of June 1, 1975), which were devised to outline the maritime boundaries of the two countries following their independence. The line emerging from those agreements was drawn through the Cross River estuary west of the peninsula, thereby implying Cameroonian ownership over Bakassi. However, Nigeria never ratified the agreement, while Cameroon regarded it as being in force.

4. The ICJ delivered its judgment on October 10, 2002, finding (based principally on the Anglo-German agreement) that sovereignty over Bakassi did indeed rest with Cameroon. It instructed Nigeria to transfer possession of the peninsula,

but did not require its inhabitants to move or change their nationality. Cameroon was thus given a substantial Nigerian population and was required to protect their rights, infrastructure, and welfare.

E. Politics, post-ICJ Decision

1. The verdict caused consternation in Nigeria, arousing vitriolic comment from Nigerian officials and media alike. Chief Richard Akinjide, a former Nigerian Attorney-General and Minister of Justice, who had been a leading member of Nigeria's legal team, described the decision as "50% international law and 50% international politics, "blatantly biased and unfair", and a "complete fraud." The Nigerian newspaper The Guardian went further, declaring the decision was "a rape and unforeseen international conspiracy against Nigeria's territorial integrity and sovereignty" and "part of a Western ploy to foment and perpetuate trouble in Africa."

2. The immediate outcome of the controversy was a de facto Nigerian refusal to withdraw its military from the peninsula and cede sovereignty to Cameroon. The Nigerian government did not, however, openly reject the verdict, but instead called for an agreement that would provide "peace with honor, with the interest and welfare of our people."

3. The ICJ's judgment was backed up the UN. Secretary-General Kofi Annan intervened as mediator and chaired a tripartite summit with the two countries' presidents on Nov. 15, 2002, which created a mixed commission to facilitate peaceful implementation of the ICJ's decision. A further summit was held on January 31, 2004.

4. The process was complicated by Bakassi inhabitants' resistance to the transfer of sovereignty, including threats to secede and a decision to seek independence reportedly made on July 7, 2006. That decision was announced by militants of a "Bakassi Movement for Self- Determination" (BAMOSD), the Movement for the Emancipation of the Niger Delta (MEND), and a southern Cameroon group, the Southern Cameroons Peoples' Organization (SCAPO).The militants' declaration had no further consequences, though it did alert both governments to continuing unhappiness among Bakassi residents.

5. On June 13, 2006, Biya-Obasanjo talks at the UN resulted in a final resolution of the conflict, with Nigeria agreeing to abide by the ICJ's judgment under the terms noted in D7 above.

6. I think it more than likely that the final agreement came about also because both sides realized that maintaining the conflict had little payoff for them and might lead to further damaging, unforeseen political and economic costs. Nigeria clearly had other more pressing issues to confront, and Cameroon understood not only that it had the better diplomatic and legal hand, but that cooperation with an accommodating Obasanjo regime - a position quietly pushed by the multinational oil companies, who operate transnationally across the Cameroon-Nigeria border - benefited both sides.

7. The initial negative Nigerian reaction was not unanticipated, and perhaps even helped along by the Nigerian government as a way to let angry Nigerians blow off steam after the ICJ decision. That the Nigerian did not reject ICJ's

decision offhand, and then later came around after soothing intervention by the UN and Annan speaks to its ultimate resolve to settle the matter once and for all.

F. Lessons from the Bakassi Dispute

1. The dispute, ongoing since 1961, fortunately never became central to the politics of either Nigeria or Cameroon; had it so become, as it could have during the military confrontations between 1993 and 1996, it would have been much more difficult to resolve. [Perhaps one way of finding resolution to a conflict is first for both sides to agree to reduce it in size ("after all, it's really not all that important to us" - I recall someone talking about "letting the hot potato cool down")]

2. Lesson #1 notwithstanding, because the dispute involved both a conflict over resources and territory, it became more complicated, and thus took longer to resolve. And that, because a zero-sum solution to either part was simply unthinkable, at least from the standpoint of both parties: Bakassi was indivisible, as were the oil/gas resources in contention. It is true that resources fought over become more desirable the longer the conflict, and that territory assumes iconic proportions when linked with nationalism, but it remains that confronted separately, or serially, resource and boundary/territorial conflicts may be thus somewhat easier to resolve.

3. To all intents and purposes, Cameroon and Nigeria fought each other to a draw- politically and militarily - in this dispute, to the point that a combination of political accommodation on both sides (Obasanjo plus Biya) and the

opportunity for a face-saving intervention (ICJ and the UN) could produce, more or less, win-win outcome. (To be sure, Cameroon came out materially ahead in the affair, but Nigeria in fact lost little and gained considerable face and political good will in the bargain.)

G. A Timeline of the Dispute

Ca. 1450: Efik "kingdom" founded in Bakassi, subsequently incorporated into "kingdom of Old Calabar

Sept. 10, 1884: British Treaty of Protection with Kings and Chiefs of Old Calabar, giving British control over entire Old Calabar territory, including Bakassi.

1885 onward: Anglo-German correspondence on Nigeria-German Kamerun border issues

April 12, 1913: Anglo-German Agreement defining spheres of control in German Kamerun-Nigeria border region, including Bakassi.

July 10, 1919: "Milner-Simon Declaration" defining limits of French and British (League of Nations) Mandates created after WW, plus clarifications in 1929, 1930, and 1931

.

December 13, 1946, U.N. General Assembly approves Trusteeship agreements including boundary definitions per Milner-Simon Declaration (and subsequent clarifications).

1960: both Cameroon and Nigeria accede to independence on basis of boundaries inherited from previous period.

August 14, 1970: Cameroon & Nigeria agree to form Joint Boundary Commission and work on delimiting southern maritime and onshore boundaries (Yaoundé Declaration I)

April 4, 1971: Yaoundé (Heads of State) Declaration II agrees on new Nigeria-Cameroon maritime border delimitation, including Bakassi as part of Cameroon

June 1, 1975: Maroua Declaration clarifies Nigeria-Cameroon southern border, including Bakassi as part of Cameroon.

1967-70, Nigerian civil war: Biafran refugees in Bakassi (and western Cameroon)

1976-79: First Cameroon license contracts to international oil/gas companies re hydrocarbon explorations offshore and onshore near Bakassi

1977-81: sporadic Cameroon-Nigeria military clashes in/around Bakassi

1993: Nigeria seeks military solution to dispute, occupies Bakassi, which results in military clashes with Cameroon forces, casualties and property damage; no winners

March 29, 1994: Cameroon takes Bakassi & and other border issues to International Court of Justice; Court agrees to accept Cameroonian application

1996, February: Further military confrontations; no winners

Oct. 10, 2002: ICJ delivers its judgment, awards Bakassi to Cameroon, defines maritime boundaries between Nigeria & Cameroon in Gulf of Guinea and other Cameroon-Nigeria border issues

June 13-16, 2006: Biya and Obasanjo meet at UN under auspices of SG Annan, agree on final resolution of conflict

July 7, 2006: (Anglophone) Cameroonian, Bakassi, Nigerian militants declare Bakassi independence; nothing comes of declaration.

August 16, 2006: formal ceremony handing over northern part of Bakassi to Cameroon begins process of implementing ICJ judgment

H. Questions Posed by various colleagues:

1. *Origins of the dispute?* See above, H, "History ..."

2. *Why was there a political will to settle by arbitration?* See above, E, "Post ICJ politics," #6 and 7, and F, "Lessons ...".

3. *Current relations between Nigeria and Cameroon?* So far, so good. Relations appear to be good, even cooperative. Much depends on the implementation of the final Biya-Obasanjo agreement, which appears to be going smoothly, by the new Nigerian government. I've not seen anything that suggests otherwise.

4. *Lateral, collateral impact of Bakassi dispute on various conflicts in Nigeria & Cameroon?* See above E4. MEND (Delta group) and SCAPO (Cameroon secessionist group)

intervention to threaten secession and declaration of a Bakassi independence appear to have been opportunistic attempts to upset the ICJ decision and Biya-Obasanjo entente and gain further attention to these groups' activities and demands. I doubt if these interventions have any further legs or impact, given these groups' own concerns and play within their own Nigerian and Cameroonian political spaces.

5. *Similarities (to Horn)?* (a) Both the Nigeria-Cameroon boundary problems appear to rest, when put to legal test, on colonial-period agreements/treaties/conventions; (b) the longer such disputes last, the greater the temptation to resolve them by military force, as witness the 1993-97 Bakassi confrontation and the Ogaden, and Eritrea-Ethiopian wars; (c) in neither cases did questions of self-determination either play an important role, or if evoked (as by Somalia), were used as regime justification for aggression.

6. *Regional and territorial linkages?* The ICJ judgment involved the interests of Equatorial Guinea (re the maritime boundary) and those of Niger and Chad as it affected the latter countries in relation to the Chad Basin Delimitation Treaty, thus far ratified only by Cameroon and Nigeria.

7. *Legacies of previous wars?* See above, #5. The boundaries themselves are the result of both the legacies of the colonial wars and colonial-period agreements; however, by common agreement in Africa, those boundaries remain more or less sacrosanct, changed only by force majeure (e.g., the Eritrean secession, demarcation of the Tanzania-Uganda border long after the unsuccessful Ugandan invasion of Tanzania in 1978) or through long contention and/or negotiation.) The only other instances of relevance are the 1974 Mali-Burkina Faso

war, briefly resumed in 1986, over border claims by both states, and the 1973 annexation of Aouzou by Libya, eventually frustrated by joint French-Chadian military operations and saw Aouzou awarded to Chad by the ICJ. In 1983, after an OUA mediation commission found itself stymied on the Mali-Burkina issue, the matter went to the ICJ, which in effect decided to halve the claims. Both sides rejected the decision, and briefly resumed the war in 1986. To date, the matter has not been finally settled.

8. *Mediation efforts and other CR interventions in Bakassi dispute?* From mid-1960 on, the Joint Cameroon-Nigeria Border Commission tried to help resolve the Bakassi dispute, but very little was achieved. Mediation by Togo's President Eyadema (on behalf of the OAU) and the adoption of resolutions by the UN and the OAU did little to move the issue to resolution. The matter was then taken to the ICJ in March 1994. The next significant intervention occurred on 5 September 2002, a month before the Court's verdict, UN S-G Annan, in the presence of French President Jacques Chirac, brought Biya and Obasanjo together to pledge compliance with the Court's verdict. Though the initial Nigerian reaction was negative, continuing pressure by the UN and the OAU/AU, plus the facts on the ground, permitted the final Biya-Obasanjo meeting and its agreement to end the dispute.

9. *Mauritanian, Chadian, Niger roles?* Niger and Chad, in relation to the ICJ decision, and no information on any Mauritanian role, save through the OAU/AU.

H. Bibliography

Reliable (and non-partisan) materials on the Bakassi dispute are generally sparse; the most reliable sources are the 2005 Konings article and the discussion of the various claims in the 2002 ICJ decision (see below). I consulted the following materials, plus several recent news reports, in preparing this summary:

Beckker, Pieter H.F., 2003, "Land and Maritime Boundary Between Cameroon and Nigeria (Cameroon v. Nigeria; Equatorial Guinea Intervening)," *American Journal of International Law*, Vol 97, No. 2 (Apr., 2003), pp. 387-398.

Biakolo, Francis, 2005, "Au-déla du verdict de la CIJ," *Africa Express* No. 013 (Nov., 2005), p.31.

"Bakassi," *Wikipedia,* June 2006

Energy Information Administration (US Dep't of Energy), "Chad and Cameroon," Background, Oil, Natural Gas, etc., Country Analysis Brief, December 2004

Ifesi, Adaeze, 2004, "Offshore delimitation of resource deposits situated across national boundaries: The International Court of Justice decision in Cameroon v. Nigeria lending clarity or compromise?" *Transnational Dispute Management*, Vol. I, issue #01, Feb. 2004.

International Court of Justice, Year 2002, "Case Concerning the Land and Maritime Boundary Between Cameroon and Nigeria (Cameroon v. Nigeria: Equatorial Guinea Intervening)," General List No. 94, 10 October 2002.

Konings, Piet, 2005, "The Anglophone Cameroon-Nigeria Boundary: Opportunity and Conflicts," *African Affairs*, 104/415 (2005), pp. 275-301.

Naldi, Gino, 1986, "Case Concerning the Frontier Dispute Between Burkina Faso and Mali: Provisional Measures of Protection," *The International and Comparative Law Quarterly*, vol 35, no. 4 (Oct, 1986), pp. 970-975.

Ntemfac Nchwete Ofege, 2004, "Oil Politics Around the Bakassi Peninsula," *Post Watch*, 2004.

"Recent Developments in Oil and Gas Law in Cameroon," *Oil and Gas Law* (The Nico Halle & Co Law Firm, Douala, Cameroon, 2006(?))

Sumner, Brian Taylor, "Territorial Disputes at the International Court of Justice," 53 *Duke Law Journal* 1779 (2006?)

Total/Total E&P Cameroon, "Financial Transparency, Total in Cameroon," June 2006

I. Recommendations

1. **Implementing Biya-Obasanjo agreement:** Full implementation of the final agreement on Bakassi negotiated by Biya and Obasanjo and mediated by Kofi Annan in June 2006 is crucial. Complete withdrawal of Nigerian troops and officials from Bakassi, to be completed in 2008, should be monitored by the UN or some other appropriate body, such as the AU.

2. **Border security:** Security forces on both sides of the new frontier should be limited to such police/security personnel needed for ordinary supervision of the border, including crossing control (immigration, visas, normal commercial passage, etc.), customs supervision, anti-smuggling operations, etc.

3. **Protection of Bakassi residents' rights:** Monitoring the Nigerian withdrawal should be paralleled by monitoring (by the Mixed Commission?) of Cameroon's obligation to protect the rights of the Bakassi inhabitants, and that supervision to extend beyond the 2008 withdrawal deadline.

4. **Citizenship, nationality protection:** A key Cameroonian obligation is to protect the nationality/citizenship rights of the Bakassi inhabitants. Possible Cameroonian move to pressure Bakassi residents to take Cameroonian citizenship – or in extremis, to legislate or simply mandate such citizenship – should be vigorously resisted by the monitoring agency, but without prejudice to voluntary change in citizenship by the inhabitants themselves.

5. **Development:** Cameroon announced its intention to create an eco-tourist area in Bakassi (Financial Times, July 12, 2007, Nigeria insert); that should be encouraged, so long as the rights of the Bakassi inhabitants are respected and the project itself is monitored to that end. Similarly monitoring should accompany oil/gas exploration and/or production on the peninsula.

6. **Settling outstanding border disputes:** The record shows that resolution of African boundary, and other interstate disputes occurs more often when the parties avail themselves of good offices, mediation, arbitration, and other conflict resolution modalities offered or available by international organizations, friendly/neutral parties, or NGO's dedicated to such resolution. A considerable body of international law, treaty law, comity, and convention already encourages, or mandates, such resolution. War or other armed action to settle such disputes more often than not resolves little, leave residues of antagonism on both sides, or encourages extremist elements on both sides. (The military confrontations of 1993-97 in/around Bakassi settled nothing, made peaceful settlement more difficult.) For current disputes, see World Factbook list.

Conclusion

This volume has followed Victor Le Vine from just past the age of thirty, as a doctoral candidate investigating the anatomy of Cameroon's emerging new state, to a front line scholarly niche as he approached eighty. Each text included here would have been of interest and utility for a wide range of contemporaries when it was written, and continues to be so in the present.

Chapters 1 and 2 recounted how Cameroon became independent and (re)unified, and showed the flaws and fault lines that have made its statecraft difficult and its statehood at times precarious, especially when ethnic group, language community and constitutional issues flare up. Those flaws and fault lines remain in place, and play. Anglophone secessionists in the Southern Cameroons National Council, banned since it consolidated and strengthened their movement in the mid-1990s, persist at home and among European and North American migrants including political asylum refugees, supported by observer status in United Nations agencies for marginalized minorities. Both nominally legal but often harassed political parties like (most prominently) the Social Democratic Front and civil society interest groups maintain domestic opposition within and across ethnic group and language communities, and contest the constitution. Against the state authority's insistence that its governance apparatus has ensured public order during decades when turmoil has destabilized many of Cameroon's neighbors, they cite corruption, economic stagnation, electoral fraud, environmental degradation, human rights violations, information control, public sector monopolies and 1996 constitutional amendments never truly activated. The opposition, though fatigued and muted by the regime's incumbency and its own mishaps and credibility gaps, continues to protest conventional politics and the Cameroon state's scaffolding, and is echoed by international agencies like Amnesty International, Human Rights Watch, Transparency International and Reporters Without Borders.

Chapter 3, Le Vine's 1980 ambassadorial briefing emphasizing the need for Cameroon to be "seen from below," marked his evolving perspective on its governance. Chapters 4 and 5, his 1984 and 1992 "crisis" texts, incorporated such ground level factors where timely, and provided commentaries on and comparisons between Ahmadou Ahidjo and Paul Biya. The 1990-1992 upheavals failed to produce the democratic "succession" or "transition" that Le Vine surmised was possible at the time; the movement's collective oppositional vigor stalled by 2000 and has weakened since. But these texts are uniformly instructive on the grievances for which Cameroonians still seek publicity and redress at home and abroad. Le Vine's 1984 and 1992 bills of particulars on the conduct of Cameroon's public life and his questions about the presidential succession from Ahidjo to Biya have their place in the reckoning as Biya's presidency reaches its fourth decade and the succession issue looms large again.

Chapter 6 reviewed Ahidjo's career and now invites further, comparative speculation on the "legacy" scholarship that will evaluate Biya's presidency. Chapter 7's parapolitics theme added local texture to national politics. Chapter 8's Bakassi text briefed readers on Cameroon's future energy policy deliberations as part of its statecraft, and its regional diplomacy, in ways that apply to its own and other African countries' futures.

Victor Le Vine's short writings on Cameroon reflected his own youthful experience in trilingual and trinational transit, his academic training to 1960, and Cameroon's experience as he studied and weighed it thereafter. The country-specific texts fully reproduced here and the brief Cameroon excerpt drawn from *Politics in Francophone Africa* balanced the priorities of and tensions between local and national governance, the maintenance of order and the expansion of liberties, and the perennial interplay of continuity and change. His scholarship, focused first on Cameroon's birth as a sovereign nation-state, matured over half a century's course and became keenly attuned not just to the state's governance but also to the contours of civil society closer to the Cameroonian population's claims for freedoms in terms that younger scholars elaborated during that interval. Victor's learning and style registered in his close scrutiny of Cameroon's institutions and personalities, and in the intricacy of his own narratives and analyses. Encountering his work selected here, both those who have followed the country's scholarship since independence and those new to it will recognize both a young pioneer's path and an elder master's voice and touch.